Sounding Heaven
and Earth

David H. W. Grubb is Chief Executive of The SPIRE Trust. Formerly a headteacher, he has held senior appointments at a number of major charities: Barnardo's, Feed the Children and Children's Aid Direct.

The SPIRE Trust is an interdenominational Christian charity established to support secondary schools in providing a range of stimulating experiences of living Christian practice and values. It does this through dance, drama, art, music and creative writing in conferences and workshops for pupils.

By the same author

Published prose includes:
Beneath the Visiting Moon (Anthony Mott Ltd, 1983)
Sorry Days Are Over (Square One, 1990)
Sanctuary (Stride, 1997)

Published poetry includes:
The All Night Orchestra (Loxwood Stoneleigh, 1994)
Turtle Mythologies (Salzburg, 1994)
An Alphabet of Light (Oversteps, 1999)
Conversations Before the End of Time (Dionysia, 2001)
The Man Who Thought He Was (Tern, 2000)
The Memory of Rooms (Stride, 2001)
The Elephant In The Room (Driftwood, 2004)

Sounding Heaven and Earth

New Voices in Prayer

Compiled by

David H. W. Grubb

CANTERBURY
PRESS
Norwich

in association with

The
SPIRE
Trust
Supporting Pupils In
Religious Education

First published in 2004 by the Canterbury Press,
Norwich (a publishing imprint of Hymns Ancient &
Modern Limited, a registered charity)
St Mary's Works, St Mary's Plain,
Norwich, Norfolk, NR3 3BH

www.scm-canterburypress.co.uk

British Library Cataloguing in Publication data

A catalogue record for this book is available from the
British Library

Illustrations by Robbie Mills and Mary Matthews.
Front cover illustration by John Rowlands-Pritchard.

ISBN 1-85311-569-X

Typeset by Regent Typesetting
Printed and bound by
Biddles Ltd, www.biddles.co.uk

Contents

Foreword

One of the most poignant requests uttered by the disciples to Jesus was 'Teach us to pray'; and in one way or another that request is still heard daily, in and out of the Christian Church. We still stand in desperate need of resources that will tell us something of what prayer is and isn't – its varieties and 'seasons', its vehicles in word and image, art and dance, its many possible locations, its own ebbing and flowing into silence.

So here is an anthology which tries to do some justice to the variety of prayer, to both its accessibility and its challenge and mystery. I am very glad to commend it as part of the work of The SPIRE Trust in its outreach to young people and to those who seek to teach and guide them. I hope it will open many doors, not only into the life of prayer but also into the Christian vision and commitment that nourishes prayer.

Rowan Williams
Archbishop of Canterbury

Preface

The place of prayer and the point of praying are central to spiritual dialogue and religious experience. At the start of the twenty-first century millions of people of limited faith turn to prayer at times of personal challenge. Those who call themselves Christians regard prayer as the most basic form of celebration, supplication and setting things right with God on a daily basis.

Sounding Heaven and Earth is an anthology attempting to gather together the broadest diversity of aspiration and identity. It explores the places where we pray, the manner in which we enter prayer, the way we use words and music, art and dance and sometimes silence to explore and express with greater force.

It gives me immense pleasure to introduce this book, which demonstrates another development in the work of The SPIRE Trust, reaching out to more young people and those who teach and guide them, seeking to develop a greater awareness and understanding of Christian beliefs.

Ronald Blythe

Introduction

William Blake provides a radiant statement with which to introduce this book:

> Unless the eye catch fire
>   The God will not be seen.
> Unless the ear catch fire
>   The God will not be heard.
> Unless the tongue catch fire
>   The God will not be named.
> Unless the heart catch fire
>   The God will not be loved.
> Unless the mind catch fire
>   The God will not be known.

In these lines, these images, these rhythms, we encounter the challenge of poetry and also the potential of prayer and faith.

One purpose of this book is to share and celebrate the diversity of prayer and approaches to praying. Just where are we with our acts and occasions of prayer at the beginning of the twenty-first century? Where have the words got to when images and music, dance and drama, silence and electronic enhancement can cascade from the most simple impulse to pray?

For many of us there is still a contentment in using other people's words. Some of these words are extremely old; they provide continuity and a sense of order. We are also happy to permit another voice to express them. The communal 'Amen' acts as a sign of affirmation and ownership.

There are also more private prayers, expressed in the head,

seldom written down, half heard as we rush from this to that. It is a spiritual breathing in and out. It is just on the edge of our lives but it is real. It is mostly expressed in intuitive heart whispers, soul soliloquies. Sometimes it is a silent encounter.

The concept of non-verbal prayer, a language without text, is also deeply significant and ancient. Meditation, music, dance, sculpture, art, arrangements of the spiritual, expressions against void, the mind flying between other spaces; these also create a diversity in Christian worship as well as non-Christian faiths.

~~~~~~

Another purpose of this book is to promote voices and images from those who have the faith to be unsure, angry or stung by doubt. They also follow a long tradition. They wrestle with the fire blazing in their evocations and discourses, and the power of such endeavours is also vital. What is the place for the prayer of loss, the anger prayer, the dereliction prayer, the grief prayer, the dread prayer, the lamentation, the tares and nettles and nails and broken promises prayer?

The most poignant examples of placing the pain within the prayer or the poem, of words attempting what silence has held, is in the literature of dereliction, the Holocaust testaments, in the words of Bonhoeffer and Celan, Gershon, Wiesel and Levi. It is as if God stepped out for a while, was attending to something else and yet was totally involved. The unsigned inscription found on the wall of a cave in Cologne where Jews had been hiding is a witness and a celebration:

I Believe

I believe in the sun
though it is late in rising
I believe in love
though it is absent
I believe in God
though he is silent . . .

~~~~~~

In many cases the form of written prayer appears to be very close to the form of poems. This is not because of literary device so much as the seeking nature of the prayer. The number of poems that centre in on an expression of faith or need for faith or grasping at faith is evident in numerous magazines, poetry collections and anthologies. There is extraordinary diversity in writers such as R. S. Thomas, Jack Clemo, Robin Robertson, Carol Ann Duffy, Michael Langley, Anne Sexton, Denise Levertov, Jorie Graham, John F. Deane, C. Wright and J. A. Penalosa.

Are prayers letters to God? Can a prayer lead one to God? Are they always going to catch rays but never become the ray itself? And, again, is this where they overlap with poems? As R. S. Thomas puts it,

> Poetry is that
> which arrives at the intellect
> by way of the heart.

You can slice open these poems like you slice open an apple. There is that unique sight and insight in them that remains subtle and vulnerable and which has a magnitude of meanings. There is no end to this.

~~~~~~

In seeking to explore diversity in prayers and praying there is a need also to consider when form and order become not only the property of prayers but also the prayer itself.

Music and architecture, incantations and robes, rites and rituals have so long been the devices but when are they the essence? Could a cathedral actually be a prayer? Is the Faith House at Holton Lee, Dorset, a devout design or an actual fusion of form and faith? Could it be an act of worship? Can a building become an eye of fire? Can a garden? Can we create and then enter the icon or is this mere mystery? Are we, like Gerontius, never to get closer than the approach? Is close enough?

~~~~~~

Those who have contributed to this book have been asked to reflect on what prayer – in whatever form – means to them. Not an easy task – but then this book is not about ease. It is

INTRODUCTION

something to do with eyes and minds of fire by which God may be known and spoken to.

The title, **Sounding Heaven and Earth**, touches on wonder. Expressions of amazement, awe, praise and jubilation are particularly rousing in religious music, psalms, songs of spiritual praise, and religious rhapsodies set to music, such as 'The Daniel Jazz'. It can radiate in hymns such as 'Lord of the Dance', 'Lord, the light of your love is shining', and 'Amazing grace!', and, in a different way, in 'Be still, for the presence of the Lord', 'Cantate Domino' and 'Lord for the years'. It can reach the sublime in the human voice and organ and drums.

Prayer, therefore, is a landscape that we travel and encounter in different ways at different stages of our lives. To make meaning and gain wisdom we create spiritual places to seek, enclose and express; we make alphabets and altars and arrangements of faith. We create the sumptuous and the simple, the ornate and the ordinary, so that we might hear God and God hear us.

David H. W. Grubb
Chief Executive
The SPIRE Trust

The
SPIRE
Trust
Supporting Pupils In
Religious Education

Different Ways of Using This Book and Letting It Use You

Many readers of anthologies dip into different sections, neither anticipating nor attempting a chronological narrative. One minute you are in a quiet garden, the next within a storm.

There are seven sections: Prayers; Poetry; Points of Light; Stations; Music and Dance; Questions and Responses; and Different Voices, each with a brief introductory comment. Different Voices, at the end of the anthology, contains questions and topics for teachers, pupils, youth leaders and ordinands.

The twin objectives of the book – to celebrate spiritual diversity and to stimulate discussion – are central issues for The SPIRE Trust, working in secondary schools in the UK, and supporting pupils in Religious Education through art, drama, creative writing, dance and music.

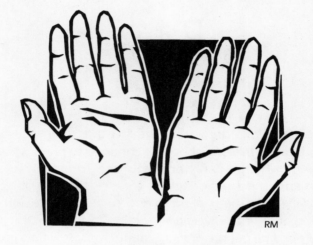

RM

DISCOVERING
FAITH
THROUGH Prayers

Prayers

This anthology grew from the fact that in an age of spiritual uncertainty millions of people continue to pray. What they are doing, why they pray and how they go about it reveals an immense spectrum of beliefs, creeds, attitudes, objectives and activities. This book seeks to encounter, explore and celebrate some of this rich diversity.

For some people prayer is about as upfront as one can get. It is like taking the gloves off, no punches pulled, ten rounds and no throwing in the towel. This is mind to mind, emotion to emotion. This is nakedness.

For other people it is always a journey, a gradual seeking, a moving forward with pauses and silences that are integral. The journey continues as long as we are alive and have the power of thought.

When we enter prayer there is often a blending of challenge and grace and need. We reveal. We receive. There is a continuum of concern and calling.

The Prayer

The prayer sometimes stands on its head,
says things you don't wish to hear,
leaves the door open.

The prayer is always on time or one step ahead,
is up at all hours,
doesn't require silence.

The prayer enters the centre of a second
and whams home its jazz or carol or
distant music that surprises you.

The prayer won't lie down flat, fit your vision,
prevent God's yawn,
accept your loud 'amens'.

The prayer never sleeps, keeps fretting,
rainbows your terror, won't go away,
does not love you.

The prayer has its own way, believes
in the power of doubt,
is no angel.

David H. W. Grubb

Shadows and Light

Lord, when shadows
enter our lives,
let your light shine through.
Let us recognise it, be comforted
and give thanks to you.

Mary H. Scott

Praise

Praise is not merely a word – it is the experience when our
    spirit joins with His
And at the exact point of meeting
There comes – from us
       A chime of bells,
       A clarion sound of trumpet notes,
       A single liquid note of joy.
From Him –
       The essence of light,
       The warmth of His glory.
Lord teach me to pray,
       Teach me to praise.
Elicit from my heart the chime of bells, that rings
       Out into the blackest of nights, and moves
       Aside the darkness.
Draw from my depths the clarion sound that
       Strengthens the weak, and gladdens the heart.
           Teach me to praise.

Jean McLellan

Faith Notes

Lord – sometimes my days stretch out like grey tracks,
       Mud underfoot, mist overhead.
Straightened on every hand by the blackness of bare trees
       Hopeless,
       Shadow-filled
       Twilight days.
And then from somewhere deep within, the Spirit-song,
Not played with notes of circumstance or outward evidence
But a quiet song of stirring hope.
Faith notes – striding ahead into the murky future and
    bringing
       Certainty – sureness.
And with the awakening of faith
       Comes an enhancement of natural sight

The same bare branches now sport raindrops of crystal
And tiny, hardly revealed buds herald
      Spring growth,
      New life.
Scarlet rosehips quicken the senses
And a solitary birdsong
Soars through the grey mist.
Lord, fill my grey days with your Spirit song.
Quicken my innermost being with the sure and certain
  knowledge
      That all my paths are known by you
      My life is in your hands
      My hope is sure.

              Jean McLellan

Buried Grain

    I stretch for the skies
    Like a grain buried
    Nurtured by your love

    I turn towards the light
    Like a plant on the sill
    Reaching to glimpse the truth of hope

    I raise my head to the sun
    Like the crops in the earth
    Scanning for the warmth of your mercy

    I sway and seek the freshening rain
    Unsure of my direction
    Searching out the waters of my baptism

    Like the mustard tree
    My branches stretch to shelter
    Reaching for ways to do your work

Compassionate God you know me
Hold me and direct me
Help me to water the seeds of your kingdom

Loving God of mercy
Justice and compassion
Guide me towards the light of your truth

Linda Jones/CAFOD

Shrovetide: A Prayer for Absolution

With clear cold sunlight breaking from the east
Cleansing the dark remains of last year's fields
    Let my soul be shriven
    All my sins forgiven.

With water from the crushing frothy stream
Brimful and icier than melted snow
    Let my soul be shriven
    All my sins forgiven.

With grass, wild garlic, coarse and green,
And daffodils now opening into heaven
    Let my soul be shriven
    All my sins forgiven.

With the abrasive caws of mounting rooks
Expelling unseen powers from the air
    Let my soul be shriven
    All my sins forgiven.

With penetrating tongues of pure blue fire
Returning flesh to its primordial light
    Let my soul be shriven
    All my sins forgiven.

James Harpur

Four Winter Antiphons

Come, Arbiter of life, of death,
come in the frost's fierce touch
to wake us out of summer drowsiness,
arresting rosebuds, curling mottled leaves
to crispness, easing the trees to sleep;
scythe through the misted air
to harden earth, to sharpen choices,
trying the appetite for life.

Come, ruthful Scrutineer
of all the heart's devices,
come in the inquisition of the wind,
tempered with blowing over icy seas,
to sweep our streets of idle loitering,
search for the gaps, for papered cracks
in our veneer; come keenest sword,
pass between joints and marrow.

Come, Guardian of the burning gates, come
but defend us from harsh punishments
of cold, from black betrayals of the ice,
the slow corruption of extremities,
the sad withdrawal of passion;
from the dulled eye of appetite,
the iron of a frozen heart, deliver us,
from nightmares of a cold, hard bed.

Come, Messenger of radiance, come
with the brilliance of new spun icicles,
drop as the purity of snowflakes,
that obscure a leaden sky,
with drifting otherworldliness,
and spread protective wings, to cover
with transfiguring dark all secret promises
of hope, eventual new birth.

Tony Lucas

A Tourist at Mass

Last night we watched a gypsy in the square
swill liquid from an old bent can, set torch
to mouth, and blow a column of bright flame
billowing far beyond him, till the night air
closed and swallowed up its tongues again.

This morning we receive the cup, tasting
the sweetness that you lend. O let the angel
now come down and touch our lips with some
live coal. Fired with your grace we too might scorch
the dark with love it could not comprehend.

Tony Lucas

Square 8g

And in the high tower church at
Probus I prayed that God might keep
you safe I was not then to know
how needful was the prayer And only later, after a long night
of sleeplessness, the price I too
had need to pay, did I become
mindful of the joyous answer

Gerald England

Prayer

Prayer is a straight line
========================
God is the track not intermediate station

Gerald England

Recension Day

Unburn the boat, rebuild the bridge,
Reconsecrate the sacrilege,
Unspill the milk, decry the tears,
Turn back the clock, relive the years,
Replace the smoke inside the fire,
Unite fulfilment with desire,
Undo the done, gainsay the said,
Revitalise the buried dead,
Revoke the penalty and clause,
Reconstitute unwritten laws,
Repair the heart, untie the tongue,
Change faithless old to hopeful young,
Inure the body to disease
And help me to forget you please.

Duncan Forbes

Iona Meditation

Along the rolling wave
Father and mother
Of endless spirit
Call in quietude
Forget-me-not
Growing close
To the yellow grass
Of this autumnal
Sacred isle.

Do not forget,
Live life's love
In tumbledown ocean
In meadowsweet
And cornflower,
Blue as the deepest
Soul kiss.

Oh I am bliss,
I am mother
And father,
I am love,
I am open,
Always open:
Come to me.

Dee Rimbaud

La Que Sabe's Bell

I grow lighter
On the wings
Of your liquid sound
And am taken
On journeys
I cannot fathom.

The clarity of you:
Messenger
To Gods and fools.

You are all-present,
Undiscriminating:

Brass,
Sharp as glass,
Like I would want to be.

You sound
And I am silent,
Listening:

The joy of you
Dancing in my skin.

Dee Rimbaud

A Prayer for Boring Times

For Megan, whose surgeon found her interesting:
a prayer for no more operations, ever.

But if there must, may she be an open and shut
textbook case. May students fall asleep on their feet
watching a procedure of such cross-eyed dullness
that the man could (though he won't) perform it with his
    teeth.

May there be no surprises, no dilemmas, no juicy tricky bits,
no fascinating puzzles. May there be no dazzling
    needlework.
Let there be no paper got from it, to astound colleagues
at conferences in Minsk, Honolulu or the Côte d'Azure;
no brilliant (but modest) article in the BMJ.

May he tell his 'nicedaydear?' wife, **Boring! boring!**
One of those days that make you wish you'd become
an estate agent – at least you'd get out and about
and poke around inside other people's houses.
Which she'd find a very tedious reply.

Meg, may you grow up in boring times.

Carole Satyamurti

Nathaniel

You saw Nathaniel beneath his fig tree.

Fig trees are rare in my city.

Do you see me at my office desk,
    On my train,
    Struggling with a painting,
    In the cinema,
    Washing up,
    Shouting at my kids?

You called Nathaniel, but I don't hear you.

Perhaps I need to listen, for
You see me everywhere.

R. G. Ferguson

His Story

If you insist I tell the truth, I went to sea to flee my family. Living in that ramshackle house by the harbour was getting me down. Okay, I didn't give much thought, any thought at all, to whether or not it was getting my wife and kids down too. She had her part-time job cleaning at the inn, and the kids seemed to delight everyone, everyone except me, that is. I'd see the boats and the ships, and hear the sailors talk about this, that and the other, and their words were like flowers in a wilderness, the ocean a magnet to my iron heart. Any road, I did it on the spur of the moment, sort of, even though I'd been thinking about it for ages. 'The Angel' was bound for Bombay, I'd had a bit too much to drink perhaps, and no, I didn't say Goodbye and thinking about it now fair wrecks my head. But what's done is done and it can't be undone. I don't know if I can ever go back. Since I've been at sea I've changed a lot and the people who knew me back then probably wouldn't know me now even if they had a mind to. I read a lot, and I've thought long and hard, and I've learned that unto the pure all things are pure, but I don't know where that leaves me. Gertrude Stein said that a rogue is a rogue is a rogue, but I swear that now my intentions are honourable and my ends of the most admirable. There is a prayer –

> 'Lord,
>
> May the Sky
> Be constant azure overhead,
> And the Ocean a murmuring
> Never melancholy friend;
> To all good wishes allow
> A flowering of fulfilment.
> May Comradeship, Loyalty,
> Love and Compassion
> Be our guides to the edges
> Of the discovered world.
> May we bear Tempest,
> Storm, Disease and Trial
> With strength and dignity,
> And should Evil threaten
> Our bow give us spines
> Of tempered steel.
> We give ourselves
> To you, Lord.'

– and The Bible bids us pray without ceasing. I do what I can. I used to wish that the cabin boy would beg to share my bed and turn out to be a girl, but no more. I pray that my life be transformed into a neural calm, and that I be granted amiable and rewarding converse with wave and star, that a mild acceptance grace my every breath. I already accept the existence of miracles in this world.

Martin Stannard

Circle Us

Celtic imagery is especially appealing to many people today. One effective image used well by David Adam in his books of Celtic prayers is that of being circled by the loving, protective presence of God. The following intercession by the Rt Revd John Pritchard needs to be read carefully, with adequate pauses between the sections, so that the repeated 'Circle us' is striking rather than irksome.

Circle us, Lord.
Circle our Church with the light of the gospel;
May we understand more of our faith and why we believe it,
May we understand more of our doubt and not be too hard
  on it,
May we commit ourselves to following you in the small details
  of our lives; in this particular fellowship, and at this
  particular time.
Circle us, Lord. Keep light within; keep darkness out . . .

Circle us, Lord.
Circle our nation with the values of the gospel.
Give to our national institutions – Government, the law, the
  health service, the unions, the Church – give them the
  values of justice, fair representation, concern for the weak,
  equal opportunities for every person.
And may the sheer generosity of your presence infuse our
  national life with hope and encouragement.
Circle us, Lord. Keep hope within; keep despair out . . .

Circle us, Lord.
Circle our family and friends with the love of the gospel.
Keep them in peace and security. Guard those of our loved
  ones who are vulnerable; strengthen those who are
  struggling; encourage those who are on the brink of
  something new. We name these, our special people, in our
  hearts now . . .
May the deep peace of the Prince of Peace keep them all.
Circle them, Lord. Keep love within; keep danger out . . .

Circle us, Lord.

Circle the sick and the bereaved in your healing presence.

There are some we know who are simply not well; some who are fearful and in pain; some who are on their last journey. Circle them now Lord, the very people we name in our hearts or aloud, circle them in the healing presence of Christ . . .

May the touch of Christ be for them the touch of wholeness and healing.

Circle them, Lord. Keep peace within; keep fear out . . .

Circle us, Lord. Our hearts, our homes, our church, our nation, our world.

Circle us, and let us never slip outside the enchantment of your grace, for Jesus' sake.

Rt Revd John Pritchard

Litany of Jesus

This litany focuses on the many names given to Jesus in the Bible, and allows prayer to engage with those dimensions of human experience that are echoed in the life of Christ. The leader can choose how much of the litany to use, and what to change, in order to make it appropriate to the congregation.

Jesus, Word of the Father, speak for those who have no voice and stand by, powerless, while others play with their lives.
Lord hear us **Lord graciously hear us**

Jesus, child of Bethlehem, remember now those children who are born to struggle, whose mothers have no milk and whose fathers have no bread.
Lord hear us **Lord graciously hear us**

Jesus, refugee in Egypt, remember those who have been terrorised out of their homes, and now try to sing their own song in a foreign land.
Lord hear us **Lord graciously hear us**

Jesus, carpenter of Nazareth, remember now those who work with their hands but see their jobs being taken over by computers and technology.
Lord hear us **Lord graciously hear us**

Jesus, teacher of Galilee, remember now those children who think they cannot learn, that success is always for someone else, that theirs is a lost cause.
Lord hear us **Lord graciously hear us**

Jesus, friend of the poor, be a friend to the invisible poor in our neighbourhood, those we never notice, the empty and lonely ones, the exhausted and silent ones.
Lord hear us **Lord graciously hear us**

Jesus, healer of the sick, remember now our broken humanity, and touch with your tender love all those who cannot trust their bodies to be whole.
Lord hear us **Lord graciously hear us**

Jesus, light of the world, remember now those whose sight is growing dim, and who fear the dying of the light.
Lord hear us **Lord graciously hear us**

Jesus, door of the sheepfold, remember now those other sheep of yours who feel the Church is not for them because they're not good enough, or can't understand the language, or don't know the entry code.
Lord hear us **Lord graciously hear us**

Jesus, bread of life, take us, pray over us, break us open and share us out, that the Church may feed and fill the world with your generosity.
Lord hear us **Lord graciously hear us**

Jesus, prophet of Jerusalem, speak judgement to our complacency, cry aloud to our disobedience, that the manipulator, the torturer, the abuser, the destroyer, may turn back to your ways of justice and peace.
Lord hear us **Lord graciously hear us**

Jesus, man of prayer in Gethsemane, remember now those who are overwhelmed by the prospect before them, and are on their knees with nowhere else to go.
Lord hear us **Lord graciously hear us**

Jesus, victim on the cross, remember well those who hang there beside you, martyrs and fools, heroes and villains, victims of murderous regimes and people who were in the wrong place at the wrong time.
Lord hear us **Lord graciously hear us**

Jesus, risen in the garden, bring us to the terror and beauty of your risen presence, that we may be an Easter people of unshakeable hope.
Lord hear us **Lord graciously hear us**

Jesus Christ, ascended Lord, work through, and watch over, our bewildered society, that the kingdoms of this world may become the Kingdom of our God and of his Christ.
Lord hear us **Lord graciously hear us**

Jesus Christ, Lord of all, sun of righteousness, rock of ages, lamb of God, living water, true vine, dayspring, messiah, Lord and King – come again, come again in glory.

Even so come, Lord Jesus.

Rt Revd John Pritchard

Today

We journey to find solace
in our faith, and daily life,
we try to keep believing
that good will come from strife,
we pray that in God's healing
will be comfort for our pain,
that slowly, with his patience
our hope will grow again.

Sandra Robinson

Shalom

SHALOM is well-being, wholeness, the binding of the spiritual and the material into a clear reality.

SHALOM is the force to seek out peace, define it, declare it.

SHALOM is harmony that has been achieved by agreement, by seeing how things relate, by a commitment to this.

SHALOM is a calm that radiates, resources, reaches out.

SHALOM is a greeting of goodness, a recognition, a value.

SHALOM does not just happen; it is made, it is deliberate.

SHALOM is what makes the hoped for holy.

The SPIRE Trust

A Child's Prayer

I am the child who lives on
the streets;
Pray for me.

I am the child in a refugee
camp;
Pray for me.

I am the child hidden away
in an orphanage;
Pray for me.

I am the child trying to find
my parents;
Pray for me.

I am the child dying of
hunger;
Pray for me.

Share your music, your
education, your riches with
me;

Share your shoes, your food,
your blankets, your fuel,
your toys with me;

Share your ideas, your
imagination, your skills,
your time, your dreams with
me;

Share your world with me.

It should be mine as well.

Children's Aid Direct

The Daily Creator Prayer

Green fields glisten at the edge of day
and moorlands mass in morning light;
beneath, the cock-crow town hums back to life,
as highways frenzy into gear;
another day to praise your God
in field or moor or ant-hill town.

> Listen, through the office-stir,
> the factory roar and clanging mill;
> listen to the meadow call
> of pipit or the skylark's trill.

And hear your Maker, man,
and intuition-woman feel your soul
stir to the morning's call.

The town and city-sprawl reveal your God
inside the market-place and mall;
beside the tingling till or check-out point;
within the eye of the computer, school-book scrawl;
at oily lathe or bench – there's God
each day to seek and glorify.

Listen, through the office-stir,
the factory roar and clanging mill;
listen to the meadow call
of pipit or the skylark's trill,

and witness daily God made manifest. Amen.

John Waddington-Feather

A Grace Before Nature

May the great rhythms of the natural world –
Winter's meditation, spring's unfurling,
Summer's flourish, autumn's grave procession,
Pulsing tides, the silent ordering
Of snow and petal, leaf and starlight, bind us
To Nature's constancy and renovation,
So our worn hearts may beat to Nature's heart
No longer lost but cradled by creation.

Susan Skinner

Palestinian Prayer

Lord don't make me a sheep that could be slaughtered by the
butcher,
And don't make me a butcher that would slaughter sheep.
Lord help me to say the word of truth in the face of the
strong,

And help me to say the word of truth to get the applause of
    the weak.
Lord if you give me money, don't take away my happiness.
If you give me power, don't take away my brain.
If you give me success, don't take away my humility.
If you give me humility, don't take away my self dignity.
Lord help me to see the other side of the picture.
Don't let me accuse my enemies that they are betrayers,
because they have a different opinion to my own.
Teach me to love people as I love myself.
Let me speak of others as I would speak of myself.
Don't let me be proud if I succeed.
Don't let me feel downhearted if I fail.
Remind me always that failure is an experience before success.
If you take away my money, leave me hope.
If you take away my blessings, leave me the blessing of faith.
If I am bad to people, give me the courage to apologise.
If people are bad to me, give me the courage of forgiveness.
Lord if I forget you – don't forget me.

Anon, translated from Arabic by Samar Sahhar

Don't Pray for Us

Don't pray for us as Palestinians or Arabs,
Don't pray for us as Israelis or Jews,
    But pray rather for yourselves,
that you may keep us in your mind
    and not dissect us in your prayers.

In your caring for others,
    God cares for you.
As you give your life to others,
    God blesses you.
As you pour out your love,
    God pours His love into you.

Samar Sahhar

For the Children

Dear Father of Mankind,
We praise you for the gift of life, for the food we receive,
for our health and education, for the teachers and doctors
and nurses who help us.

We thank you for parents and relatives and friends.
We thank you for puzzles and jokes and our ability to
understand humour.

We thank you for the great children's stories and poems that
are part of childhood.
We thank you for hands held out in trust and friendship.

Help us to be aware of the children of war; children
who are alone, children in camps and prisons, children in the
greatest need.

Children's Aid Direct

Prayers
for Anne

Lord of the Rainbow,
Lord of all imaginable colours
You are the light and shade in everything
You are the circle and the centre of our turning world.
May we come to see in all things
The fullness of Your reality
And may we come to see through each other
The fullness of ourselves in You.

᪥᪥᪥᪥᪥

Lord, the further I go in Your mystery, the less I
understand.
Help me to have faith in my unknowing and realize that life is
a miracle.

Help me to be open: to be firm and loving, resolute and at
    peace.
Help me to have the courage to be who I am in you, and
    wholly.

Lord, may we all have the courage to be who we are,
    knowing You are in us.
Help us to face the Unknown, and to know that in it Your
    Spirit and the future lives.

〰〰〰〰

I sit before you, Lord.
I sit empty.
Help me to be true to this path
And this calling.

Help me to grow as I can help others to,
To go always ahead of myself—
And never be satisfied with knowledge.
Nothing second-hand, Lord, my friend—
But each original impulse of Your shining eyes
Looking deep through mine, and smiling.

〰〰〰〰

Lord, may I be clear, may I be here this day,
May I give of my best in whatever way I'm asked to,
And may I always seek to do that.

Guide me as Your disciple,
And may I learn to follow You

                    with my head up in the sun.

〰〰〰〰

Lord, open my ears and my eyes
To see this is Your Kingdom.
Help me in my blindness,
Help me in this suffering
(wrapped tight around me)
That cannot see.

For when I see, Lord
Everything is changed:
I walk my height
And I see past the horizon
When I walk in Your Name.

Help me to surrender to the breath You are in me,
To the breath You gave me—

And not to fear and to doubt, knowing it is You.
Lord of my life, let me breathe You.

Lord, cleanse my thoughts
So I can be here in myself
As I truly am—

Lord cleanse my heart
And keep it open
Past the bitterness of pain,

Lord cleanse my body,
Make it a fit temple
For You to dwell in.

Come, Lord, come
Make my mind into a pool
                    of clear breathing water
Out of its dark broken pieces—

Come, Lord of the Rain,
Come, Lord of the Sun,
Make me of one mind with You.

May a circle of light be around us
A circle of stillness within us—

And may today be blessed
In the Name of the Lord.

Jay Ramsay

Prayer at Sheepscombe

Spirit of the wind
Breathe down over these valleys,

Spirit of the air
Breathe in our blood,

Spirit of the water
Cleanse our eyes,

Spirit of the earth
Warm our feet,

Spirit of fire
Penetrate our hearts—

Spirit of fire
Enter our minds—

Spirit of fire
Strengthen our seeing—

That we may walk in truth
On Your Living Ground.

Jay Ramsay

Credo

I believe in the rushing wind, the tremendous driving force,
the sudden shaft, the sudden shifting of light, the
     interposition,
of the Holy Spirit in these human affairs, the interpolation
of the tributaries, ponds and sources
                              the watery interfaces
water-sheds and water-forces
                         the sudden ripple of light
throwing diamonds across the water, turning
us to another quarter;
taking us round with the ebullient stream in another meander
into the presence of Godhead in these vessels of brittle clay:
the presence lighting these figures, otherwise fast
     disappearing
into a darkness deeper than any of their own making:
turning ahead of them, like the hidden water, and calling.

I believe in the wholly Other, the presence behind the mere
                              clay of Creation:
the holy and solitary Father, who created us,
                         by whom we are well met
in the terror and joy of this and every day,
in the middle of every instant
                         at the centre of every insight
at the first and the last light of this and every I.

I believe in the grace which is daily searching and reaching us
which has to be felt to be seen, accepted to be believed,
and which, denied or acknowledged, has always inhabited us
from the first wrinkle across the ocean, as it ever shall be
in the day and the night-time, out beyond night, beyond day,
in the beginning, so, now, without end,

the sudden shaft, the ripple of light, like a person beside me,
nearer than hidden water
                         turning to speak to me:
the sudden shift, the sound of the water
                                   turning.

Brian Louis Pearce

Unite Us in Christ

Dear God, we thank you that – whatever our favoured image of you – Jesus continues to have a talent for breaking out of moulds, and ever remains provocative. So, lead us away from the security of our own comfortable images of Jesus – to face the complex issues of our day.

Be with those abandoned by relatives or friends, and bring an end to divisions caused by sexism, racism, ageism, or homophobia. Protect us from irresponsible or extreme interpretation of scripture, and check our emotional responses, we pray.

Above all, challenge us afresh to progress beyond gender divisions to know the spiritual wholeness of unity in Christ.

In the grace, and empowerment, of the Holy Spirit we pray for our lives to be so transformed.

Thanks be to God.

Wendy Whitehead

Fill Us With Peace

Dear God: generous host of your universe, we rejoice that you long for us to receive of yourself – to enliven us with your good humour and your hospitality. As we sit at your feet, fill us and refill us with your Holy Spirit. Help us to be a blessing, because we trust in your Holy Spirit to help us always. Fill us with peace, hope, courage, patience and forgiveness; and with your great love that casts out fear and anxiety.

Lord Jesus Christ, Prince of Peace, we pray for the healing of nations, and for you to guide us into the ways of peace. Lead us away from temptation – from the beckoning of false gods, and from personal hang-ups or addictions.

Be with those abandoned by family or friends: direct them toward the Light of the World, that they may find an inner peace, and ultimately be made whole.

Change the hearts and minds of those inclined toward acts of violence, terror or war, we pray, and protect all whose job it is to be alert to such fear, or deal with the consequences of desperate actions.

Help us, and them, dear God to 'put peace into each other's hands, and like a treasure hold it' so that we may know that peace which passes all understanding.

Holy God, you give life to all; you meet us in our need, and bring hope to those who look to you. So, complete your work in us, and unite us through your everlasting love. In Christ's healing name, we pray.

Thanks be to God.

Wendy Whitehead

A General Thanksgiving

With joy and thankfulness, Lord God, we come into your presence today. For the inspiration of what you have been; of what you are, and will be – to each of us, we praise you and adore your name.

Living God, we thank you for your message – which speaks to us so clearly through creation. For every valley raised up; every mountain and hill made low; for the glory of the night sky; for the depth of your boundless ocean of love. We thank you too – for every part of your world and our place in it.

We give thanks for the stimulation of the ever-changing patterns of sea and sky. Forgive us when we fail to be thankful; help us renew our desire to praise you, and to trust in your purposes for humankind. We praise you that when we misuse our environment, we can be lifted out of our selfishness and greed: for you have given us Jesus Christ to be our Saviour.

Dear Parent God, help us to grow in your will; to work for a just and equal sharing of those things we take so much for granted – food, material treasures, education – and even the faith that comes from being yours. We delight that in baptism you claim us as your sons and daughters – calling us by name.

We thank you for our friends of other faiths: for all the good things we learn from each other – help us to widen our vision and share our resources, and determine to create a more peaceful and united world.

You've brought us from darkness – into the marvellous light of your gospel – ever leading us into new truth, ever renewing your mercy, and we rejoice that your will is wholeness, and health of body, mind and spirit, for all people. So, help us, we pray, both as individuals and as part of your world-wide community, to live more in harmony with your will and purposes.

Let us together feast upon the truth of a healing and loving God who is our trusted friend.

Thanks be to God.

Wendy Whitehead

SPIRE Trust Prayers

From **Alphabets of Light**

Father, we give thanks for the value of words;
Words that proclaim our faith
Words that reveal your mission
Words that challenge ignorance
Words that reach out in love
Words that call us together
Words that heal and speak peace
Words that console and discover.

The SPIRE Trust

We are dancing with The Lord.
We are singing with The Lord.

We are painters of The Lord's glory.
We are sculptors of The Lord's light.

We are drummers in The Lord's lands.
We are trumpeters in The Lord's time.

He inhabits our sonnets and psalms and songs.
He enters our portraits and portrayals and presentations.

He exists within the silences and the sounds.
His wisdom in prayers, His whispers in silences, His glory in
    galaxies.

Our amens in alphabets of light.

The SPIRE Trust

Father, give us the courage to test our faith,
give us the imagination to describe our beliefs more boldly,
assist us as we seek out, reach out, refuse to pass by,
help us to march off the map, deliver our visions;
give us the wisdom so that we know the positive value of
    silence
and become the singers of songs and the proclaimers of
    gospels.

The SPIRE Trust

Father, we give thanks for the words that have been handed
    down to us,
that have been translated, that have survived conflicts and
    superstitions and ignorance,
that rule over our own days and ways.

Help us to protect them, give us the energy to proclaim them,
give us the intelligence to promote them in our language,
in our own ways, in our places and spaces of faith and
    education.

Give us the power of words,
The wisdom of expression,
The courage of speech,
The trust of the gospels.

The SPIRE Trust

Facing the Silence

What do we as parents, adults, carers, teachers, priests,
believers, say to our children about:
war, the arms trade, landmines, asylum seekers, race hatred?

'The peace of God that passeth all understanding.'

What do we say about failed crops, pollution, famine, waste,
killing fields, those who have no land, no food, no water?

'The peace of God that passeth all understanding.'

What do we say about those who hate us, those who would
kill us: the barren, the naked, the lost, those who have no
reason to trust or believe?

'The peace of God that passeth all understanding.'

What do we say about a God or a maybe God, or a somehow
God, or a sometimes God?

'The peace of God that passeth all understanding.'

What do we say to the teenager who senses deceit, word
games, doubt, the slip of spiritual things?

Do we leave them to stew, to somehow survive, to make do?
Do we leave them to enter the silence because we gave up?

If there is silence then our children may turn to other things.

'The peace of God that passeth all understanding.'

The SPIRE Trust

Why are they so silent?
Because they have been forbidden to speak.

Why do they not dance?
Because dancing is banned.

Why do they have numbers?
Because their names have been stolen.

Why are there no children?
Because they have been taken away.

Who is that in their midst?
It is the Messiah.

The SPIRE Trust

From **Saints Sunday**

How to Paint a Saint

You need something that resembles nettles, broken wings,
coldness of caves;
treason whips, the density of derision, poisoned water,
burning books.

You need something that catches the sky at Belsen, the
snipers mind;
scaffold silence, the song of barbed wire, a single shoe.

You need to open the apple, fly the kite, be ready for angels;
expect miracles.

The SPIRE Trust

The Eight Questions	The Eight Replies
What is the colour of a saint?	A handful of stones
What is the sound of a saint?	Kettle drums
What does a saint dress in?	Knowledge
What does a saint live in?	Our world
What does a saint eat?	What is left
What does a saint drink?	Enough
What does a saint dream?	Journeys of light
What does a saint say?	Listen

The SPIRE Trust

An Advent Prayer

Dear God

We enter this season of Advent with a desire to more fully understand the events leading up to the coming of Jesus Christ.

We enter this season of preparation and celebration surrounded by gifts and aware of those people and places in our world that have so little.

We enter this season of light and optimism aware that many people have no real knowledge of it.

At this time we seek harmony, real peace, tolerance, the grace of forgiving, the power to communicate.

In our homes and at our tables we want to make the visitor welcome, we want to prepare a place for the stranger, we want to let the light of understanding embrace our lives in words and thoughts and deeds.

Amen.

The SPIRE Trust

PRAYERS

<h1 style="text-align:center">An Easter Prayer</h1>

Dear God

We enter Easter again. It is always difficult. The reality of this season can only be understood if we accept everything leading up to it. If we have heard the words of Christ again. If we have approached the Cross. If we have rolled away the stone. If we have looked into the eyes of Jesus and accepted his life and death and resurrection.

At this time of year there is rebirth surrounding us. The entire ground yields to spring. The sky lifts and days lengthen and we celebrate with prayers and hymns. It is almost as if we had seldom observed living things so keenly, so closely before.

Help us to understand this and to express it more clearly. Assist us in sharing the Easter story. Strengthen us when we stumble and cannot summon up enough imagination and faith. Be with us when we find it difficult to move on.

Be with us in our psalms and songs and rejoicing this Easter. Be with us as we contemplate the glorious. Be with us when we experience subtle silences and moments of peace.

Amen.

The SPIRE Trust

<h1 style="text-align:center">The Greatness of Creation</h1>

Lord, help me to remember,
that in the greatness of creation,
everything matters . . . even me.

Mary H. Scott

DISCOVERING
FAITH
THROUGH Poetry

Poetry

One of the many challenges facing religious verse is that there is so much poetry within the spiritual domain already. The Bible, the Prayer Book, the ritual and the architecture provide poetry that is tried and tested and trusted. Contemporary poetry is rarely quoted, seldom trusted and not seen as an essential energy. There is another problem: there is a popular perception that a poem has to mean to be and that a religious or spiritual poem should give voice as clearly as the words to a beloved hymn.

That some of the great hymn-writers had moments of doubt – Cowper, for example – and that they were capable of obtuse phrases and cluttered metaphors does not appear to be a problem. That some were original beyond the comprehension of their readers was also not a problem.

George Herbert, Christopher Smart and William Blake all discovered and declared poems in a language that regularly overcame cautious cadences. In their work there are leaps into the light, enormous wellings up of energy and sometimes not only fabulous but also surreal passages quite beyond the normal power of words. At these moments they suggest a totally new view of earth and heaven.

Faced with such a rich tradition the poems in this anthology are selected because they express spiritual things in today's language. What they say challenges exactly because they have not been settled by time and generations of readers. They are being spoken now.

Creature Christmas

Ox:
This night I dream of green
of food and freedom.
In the dream there's light,
like the shine
from this man-scrap
with two legs short
but ten curled toes.
No rods on back, no smell
of fear to come.
Not this night.

Ass:
Each night brings bone-ache
mine have ached
from weight on back.
Tonight I'm horse-fleet
full with future, but
shot through by pain
huge as my ears,
hearing cries
from this hairless one.
But tomorrow's a hill
we needn't climb yet
he and I
when it shouts death
for beyond this night
day is at peace.

Camel:
Where I carry man and load
life's a white glare
for a four-foot slave.
The ship of me rolls
to a fiery wind
and though I may
be driven out
on a sea of sand

chokingly drowned
I shall surface
under a bluer sky
where this child
swims and asks
no slave but love.
Tonight's for praising.

Anne Born

Faith

The oak is a tower,
    each branch a muscled arm,
each leaf a word. The trunk
    rests on roots that keep faith
in the dark soil of nurture.
    An actor in the theatre of seasons:
kindling of first leaf, modest flower,
greens of summer sheltering fruit
    and the drop of acorns diving
into waiting ground.
    Then, branches stripped for cold,
gale and snow, growth goes on
    in earth and at twigs' end,
until the holy circle joins.

Anne Born

Carol

Holly pricks and stabs
    Ivy creeps and chokes
        but the white rose
lives and glows

Holly shines dark green
    Ivy twines and bends
        but the white rose
asks nothing

Holly dries and cracks
   Ivy browns and withers
      while the white rose
unfolds life

Holly is hard and dry
   Ivy's trunk binds
      but the white rose
flowers dies flowers.

Anne Born

Garden in March

The trees are bare
but not empty.
Last year's nests
and small, pouch-like
spider webs,
each filled
with what might be
winter's last snow,
are decorative reminders
that nature
is womb and tomb.

In March
the garden
straddles them.
Last summer's stalks
protrude crazily,
this summer's growth
emerges furtively
through the mulch.
I am not sure
whether the roses
are alive or dead.

In March
gardens are shy things
that need befriending.
This is not the time

to dig and disturb.
This is the season
to let roots grow down,
to wait for the pattern
unfolding in the seed,
to cultivate the capacity
for wonder.

B. Shurston

Chartres Cathedral

The spires
lean into the air
touch the blue inside
of the sky

lightly
a philosophy

a cathedral
about to lift the world
off its knees

Katherine Gallagher

Put Your Hands into Fire

The magic of hands
is rarely celebrated

Test your hands
on the heart's edge

The music of hands
is born in flame

the instinctive touchstone reaching
finally beyond fire
beyond sign-language

to shore each blending
unique as a leap into light

Katherine Gallagher

The Long Reach Out of War

They will keep restoring the glass
in broken cathedrals

to carry the eye and the colours
that were shattered

They will keep restoring the stone
in bombed cathedrals

to carry the face and the idea
that were crushed

They will keep carrying the burden
of destroyed cathedrals

even as the ashes blow back

Humanity
keeping faith with itself
even as the ashes blow back

Katherine Gallagher

Numinous

Not in the golden cloth upon the altar
but in the cracked stone patterns of the floor;
not in the gracious spacing of the pillars
rather in shadows round a vestry door.

Not in the polished ornamental woodwork
but in the worn grain of an awkward chair;
not in the colours of a stained-glass window
rather as sunlight piercing dusty air.

Tony Lucas

Window

Winter morning,
the sun springs into your eyes,
and the sky looks upside-down;
pastel clouds fan out above a wide
stretched swathe of blue, punctuated
by sparkling flocks of wheeling birds.
Glittering princes, emerging
from a spell. We waken,
on days like this,
from Winter's dark enchantment.

Winter evening,
the world is almost dusk,
just the red roofs flare and flow;
the tips of stark tree branches
are brushed with transient tints.
Down dark descends,
leaving in the West
one lingering streak of light . . .
God's left a lamp on for us,
shining under Heaven's front door.

Carole Baldock

Soulful

Wholly original,
from conception to completion,
which marked the end of an era:
the Anglican Cathedral.
Almighty citadel, forbidding,
formidable, for ever, a floating island,
Heaven its backdrop, anchored
to the earth.

I'm fascinated.

Cheerfully, a voice hails me
across the street:

tall, dark and handsome
(a perfect stranger),
scarlet jacket festooned
with dreadlock ribbons,
he grins: **'It's bin there forever,
ain't gonna fall down, ain't goin' away.'**

Then he is on his way,
sauntering off
in the opposite direction

On I go.

Slowly echoing
the words of a stranger,
learning by heart:
'**It's bin there forever,
ain't gonna fall down, ain't goin' away.'**

Carole Baldock

Our Last Hope

How do you feel when the plane crashes
And the buildings tumble down?

How do you feel when you see the photos
Of debris crashing around?

How do you feel when you see the man
Frozen in his last bid for life?

How do you feel when they pick up his body
And take it to his kids and wife?

How do you feel when the searching begins
For survivors, broken and bruised?

How do you feel when the searchers collapse
Their limbs tired and over-used?

How do you feel when survivors emerge
On stretchers blinking in light?

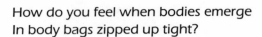

How do you feel when bodies emerge
In body bags zipped up tight?

How do you feel if your child is in there
Your brother, your sister, your friend?

How do you feel when you're told the news
Another life's come to an end?

How do you feel when you hear the dying
Their last phone call from the suicide plane?

How do you feel when no one is found
And only the dust remains?

How do you feel when you pray to the Lord
To help survivors and families cope?

How do you feel when the rubble is cleared
To extinguish or light our last hope?

Emily Dalrymple

In the Walled Garden

A reflection on the many chapels of Islay

So many stones eroded, granules of bitten grit
sheered off. The wind takes care of everything,
furnishing the moss with sharp sand, smothering
indecipherable legends in the grass. Here lieth,
there lieth . . . we guess, painful and slow,
doing our best to estimate the rest in a shadow-play
of hands, a breadth of anonymity scoured from the west.

Grains sweep in from Kilchiaran, Kilchoman
and Kilnenain, from the nameless cilla
of forgotten saints slung along the cedilla
of the Rhinns: gathering in the lap of Islay
between Gruinart and the beaches of Indaal.
Faith grows in this cradle, buffeted by superstition,
staked to the call of exile that would choke the land.

Here the gale is parried with simple deflections,
the collection of particles, painful and slow –
a putting down of roots, a kind of pioneering,
turning the past like a spit of peat,
working hidden names into a fertile tilth.
May the dead build their walls to nurture the living.
Let the living rejoice that the dead take care of themselves.

Gordon Simms

Footsteps

Each footstep
Dissolved my sorrow
As you crept gently back
Into my heart.

Replacing the fear
With joy
You opened my mind
My world to hope.

Silently praying
For this day
To be repeated
Again and again.

I paused
To count the blessings
Reflected
In your eyes.

After years of doubt
Thanking the Spirit within
For finally being able
To accept your love.

Michelle Wright

Poem for Easter

Tell me:
What came first
Easter or the egg?
Crucifixion
        or daffodils?
Three days in a tomb
        or four days
in Paris?
        (returning
Bank Holiday Monday).

When is a door
not a door?
When it is rolled away.
When is a body
not a body?
When it is a risen.

Question.
Why was it the Saviour
rode on the cross?
Answer.
To get us
to the other side.

Behold I stand.
Behold I stand and what?
Behold I stand at the door and

knock knock.

Steve Turner

He Who Would Speak

My friend came with a problem
I did not know what to say
I feared the consequence of my words
I stayed a while silent
I did not speak to my friend
My heart spoke with the Lord
The Spirit interceded and
gave me a question to ask
My friend did not answer me the question
But the Lord answered his problem

Gerald England

Into the Ultraviolet

Bees and butterflies
see beyond us, into the ultraviolet.
They scratch at colours,
representations of flowers
on a shirt or an apron,

or perhaps choose one tone,
visiting each example of it in turn
before finally giving up
and moving on.
They may never learn

the extent of their failure
but, reassured, point themselves
at the next nearest branch.
This is what I might have been thinking
in church on Sunday morning
when you thought I was praying.

Martin Caseley

Endings and Beginnings

I know where I am going,
I think.
I know where my life is taking me,
I suppose.
The way ahead is obvious,
Signposted,
A long straight run,
To where I want to be,
To be who I have planned to be,
Clearly mapped out.
My life, my will, I said.

I know where you are going,
Trust me.
Though it is not where you thought
You would be.
Listen to me, to what I say, turn around
Scary I know.
But I will hold your hand
As you choose another path
Step out into the unknown,
A new direction;
My will, He said.

I promise you this,
He said,
For every ending,
There is a beginning,
Brighter and better,
Though you may not think so,
Now.
The way ahead is clear to me,
I make the sun sear through the fog.
A new life;
My will, He said.

This is a new road for me,
Unexpected,
I'm not sure what the outcome will be,
Oh Lord.
But I know in my heart,
In my bones,
You'll be by my side all of the way,
Whatever may occur
Building a bright new tomorrow
Endings and beginnings
Your will, not my will, I said.

Beverley Jameson

Cause and Effect

Because I am tone-dumb,
Because I cannot sing
Or descant like a bird
On all or everything,
I sometimes think I have done
The next best human thing,
As if arranging words
For the inner ear to hum
Could intimate or bring
Insight into the world,
Hope of a life to come.

Duncan Forbes

A Poem

A poem
written
in blood
or bone
is not
forgotten
nor alone

in sweat
of art
and hurt
of years
words are wet
with blood
and tears

A poem
learnt
by heart
or hurt
is burnt
for comfort
in the night

and though
the makers
die and go
what the letters
say and do
can console us
dying so

console
atone
and entertain
the soul
in pain
and make us
whole.

Duncan Forbes

Dream Eclipses Reality

Yesterday I painted
Great big happy faces
On all the skyscrapers
In the Gorbals . . .
And what if skyscrapers
Really did scrape
The sky?
I would attach paintbrushes
Dripping with rainbow colours
To their radio masts
And lightning conductors.

Dee Rimbaud

The White Room

Longing for something to be different,
gather it up, jagged with discontent,

carry it to the room of complete whiteness,
white so negative, so generous

it comprehends all colours; a domain
so silent even the smallest shard of pain

falls audibly, relinquishing its hold
like a dead parasite. Take all you've railed

against, the ache of tiny consequence,
love lost, mistaken – and in that radiance

feel it dissolve, as simplifying fire
both cool and warm lets anger, fear, desire

merge with expanded light which, while it's there,
softens even the hardest facts there are.

Carole Satyamurti

Anything Could Happen

Anything could happen as you gently
without waking the others
step from the bed and move to the kitchen
open a window to breathe in the new day
the stars fading and an ant exploring the sink
undisturbed as you reach for a glass
and turn on the tap
let it all run slowly through your hands
the water   the cool air   the dawn.

C. R. Hadfield

Hope Cove

We lack songs
for these days

as the opening theme
let us say
where words fail . . .

there in the awakening of purpose
in the variations of green
on the sunlit hill
crisscrossed by walls

and above
pointing into spring
the spire
surrounded by stones
leaning this way
and that

C. R. Hadfield

To Whom It May Concern

It's September 10th
leaves are beginning to fall off trees
Early morning mists and heavy dews
Sun comes up around 6:25
I'm driving to work A couple of weeks ago
I was driving in daylight now it's headlights
                As you know I work
and part of my work is taking 999 calls
People are in trouble or dying
sometimes they're not in trouble at all
sometimes they've lost their mobile phone
Or they're just fighting neighbours
or husbands and wives This goes on always
Yesterday when I parked the car
in Crocus Street the sun was shining early
when I got back to it at 4 o'clock
rain was thumping down but 'The sun
doesn't go down It's just an illusion caused
by the world spinning round' as you know
                Last week I worked
evenings my world was turned up
side down I drove home late at night
The streets are different at night
Instead of heading for work people
are up to other stuff Scrawny tarts
loiter on Forest Road pubs chip shops
drink and some dope I suppose I was
too tired to care I wanted to be at home
                At home Ruth was asleep
I had a whisky to unwind Some
of the people I work with were still
at work taking 999 calls There is trouble
and dying sometimes there's no
trouble at all though it seems like there is
as you know And as you know
this little diary jotting is not even a scratch
on the surface of anything Ruth is asleep

I envy her Music is playing I envy it
I try to write a poem and fail
as darkness falls It was going to say how
all my poems are a reaching for something
even though I don't always know what
                    the something is

Martin Stannard

Paying Attention

To everything you say. To everything
you do. To everything. To the movement of
the day. To the still of the night.
To the music of the spheres. To the television.
To changes in the light. To what's
going on. To the pleasantries. To unfinished
business. To smoke curling into the twilight air.
To how the words lay side by side
on the page and in bed with one another.
To how easy it is to say. To how unfair
things can be. To the words and the harmony.
To that colour next to this colour and
what goes off between them. To
the particular phrasing of the question.
And working out who is in control
of the situation. And realising your own
perfections and imperfections. And
understanding that if you don't
you'll come off second best. How you'll
miss what happens when that collides
with that other. How you'll miss
the opportunity of a lifetime. The woman
in a million. And knowing you might die
any minute and so you should enjoy
what you have and notice what's there.
That it's corny but true. How paying attention
to everything is impossible but thinking it
possible is one of the finest delusions.

Martin Stannard

Why I Am Happy to Be in the City This Spring

for creepers etched
    across a wall
    like the marble veins
    on **David**'s hands;
for the lichen, moss
    & granite blocks
    of the city's ancient
    battlements;
for empty paint pots,
    loose blue string
    & 'slightly sparkling'
    bottled water
    discarded in the bushes,
    its dregs – quite still –
    reminding us
    we're only passing through;
for a builder's skip
    of silver crucifixes;
for sunlight on the golden rooster
    of a weathervane;
for a metal dragon listening
    to the jingle of cash
    in a pocket
    outside the new café;
for students drinking coffee,
    their notes taking off
    in the wind – **ta-da**!
for birdsong
    when a door slams;

for birch trees
    like Elizabethan ladies
    painted white;
for the burgeoning stems
    of Aloe Vera
    in municipal gardens
    like chubby children
    playing **Stuck-in-the-Mud**;
for water in a concrete pond;
for reflections,
    fish
    & ripples
    over grey;
for buttercups emerging
    through drain holes;
for garden planters
    standing bare all Winter,
    now filled;
for hills in the distance;
for the balm of a snail's track
    on galvanised railings
    at midnight;
for the quiddity of skyglow –
    this ongoing twilight
    from streetlamps –
    over our new home
    and, through it,
    the relief of seeing
    single stars.

Andy Brown

In Love We Sense the Briefness of Our Lives

like a shoreline seen from sea—the promise
of home and then, unsure, becoming
ever-distant like a ripple that stems from
a dropped stone; and yet it seems the past is
close behind, like the boy & girl who
entertain their parents' guests, reluctantly,
when all they've ever dreamed about is changing
themselves into animals or birds, lured
by the siren of the unseen horizon and the stories
people tell of their journeys beyond it;
lured by the migration of butterflies—
departing like leaves falling upwards
out of the shadows and into the light—
searching everywhere for signs of grace.

Andy Brown

Iona

I came too late
                at the appointed time
a chapel on a windy hill
                to meet your echo
blue peace and yearning sky
                I reach for you
Celtic crosses, seaworn stone
                aching places of our hearts
shore of silver sand
                music is the only language
wombsound and cradle song
                the day unravels
seasound and grave song
                codes and uncodes suspend time
words rise up as though
                pressed from hidden places
        time does not do this on purpose

Angela Topping

She Considers Sea Burial

Beloved Wife, Rest in Peace,
legends among slanting stones,
Never . . . in a wall of broken words.

No slow and useless mouldering for her.
She wants to suckle herring and wear
an overcoat of tweedy plaice.

Angela Topping

Tending the Plot

Of all human activities, apart from the procreation of children,
gardening is the most optimistic and hopeful.

Susan Hill

On her knees she toiled
the narrow allotment of sour soil
shovelled above her parents' coffins.
Her fingers teased out roots.

I was sent to fetch water,
to rinse green scum from the jar
where flowers were left to die.

Now she's buried there herself,
husband's ashes at her halted feet.
The plot's full and snug as families,
the black stone chock-a-block with facts.

I'm bent-backed elsewhere,
uprooting weeds, fumbling seed,
coaxing from the damp earth
all the colour and the scent I can.

Angela Topping

The Least Thing

Stone and
olive wait you
in the garden.
Sacred to you
the shrub, earth and
stone each time we
go in.

Sacred
head, stone, earth in
the garden, word
in the wind, we
are wounded, if,
thank goodness, not
like you.

Easter
always does this
to us: breaks us
down, rebukes us,
remakes our mean-
ing, rebakes us
like loaves.

Out of
the oven, fur-
nace, we emerge
yelling. What news?
That the least thing
we touch now is
holy.

Brian Louis Pearce

Lines to Jesus

Lines to Jesus are never engaged
No call back required
No answering machine
No 'press 1 for advice and 2 for confession'.
Lines to Jesus are always free
No appointment required
No hour inconvenient
No charge for late night calls.
Lines to Jesus have no time limit
There's no eye on the clock
One ear half listening
No faraway look or distracted attention.
Lines to Jesus are always connected
No dial-up needed, no busy dot.com
No password recalling
No download to wait for.
Lines to Jesus are open and waiting
So call him now . . . he is longing to hear from you.

Heather Walker

Funerary Monuments, Aegina

Simple enough distinction. The dead
always seated, the living standing by.

What complicates is how they're linked,
each couple holding hands in such
a definite, tender way it's easy to imagine
love streaming through the veins,
tingling in the fingertips. And not just that.

Standing here among the excavated tombs
in fields of snaky asphodels, you gravitate
towards some threshold, the singular step
between the now and then of everything
you ever thought was possible in life and death.

Even in those monuments that time's
been savage with and left as shadowy iconography,
there seems to be, however faintly, some purpose
flowing in the graininess of stone
hating annulment, endings of any kind.

Matt Simpson

The Song of Caedmon

And God said:
sing me somewhat, Caedmon.

I would have sung the mullet and whiting
shoaling at Whitby, the occasional porpoise
that breaks a summer horizon, the pigs
and goats poked into market.
I'd have had men listen
to new songs at harp-passings,
sung the wondrous windwork of gulls.

But God thought otherwise, sold me on dreams:
sing me Creation, Caedmon, the song
that's acceptable, that does me some credit.

So I the uneducated
was saddled with miracle; big words
broke on me, a galeforce of syllables
swept up from nowhere. I would have welcomed
a start nearer home, a local beginning.

But God thought otherwise:
work on my handiwork, carve it on crosses,
sing in Northumbrian the way the world got to
this bleak point of history. Sing to the mindful,
make me some worship.

I would have started the other way round,
charting our wonders, the wonders about us,
the disorder of gulls in a pleasure of words,
the glint of the mullet, the pigness of pigs.

Matt Simpson

Touching Truth

Thomas
touching bloodied scar
touched truth.

Trying to tighten
his grip on fact
tried touching truth.

Tormented
Thomas
needed to know

trusted
to touch
for his proof:

a question
of sins
and scars

a matter
a moment
a maybe . . .

Touching the truth
slipped past faith
into knowledge

the balance
of trust
disturbed:

denied
the possibility
of doubt . . .

scarred
for life
with belief . . .

blood and brain
never letting
wonder alone again.

Thomas
touching
truth

tormented
by
truth.

Rupert M. Loydell

Gregorian Chants

This music
walks on air

all the way
to heaven

Rupert M. Loydell

Visitation

'Angels will remain
misprints that can't be deleted.'

'Down There', Eugenio Montale

Beyond the parted curtain,
in the chalk light of morning,
an angel enters the garden.

He is a misprint, a smudged
kiss of light and shadow
in the angles of distance;

a religious device
used to talk about heaven;
a metaphorical messenger.

He is an impossibility
caught in the wind
that blows belief away,

driving angels into empty yards,
seeking sanctuary (I glimpsed
his wings in the moonlight).

I saw an angel. He will
not be dismissed, stays
hidden, as a doubt, a fiction:

one that simply cannot be.

Rupert M. Loydell

Holy Places

Somewhere to rest
where a leaf and
silence are all
waiting there.

Rupert M. Loydell

A Place

In the night the snow came,
silent and still, like the answer to a prayer,
and for a time it changed everything:
the way they lived, the way they thought.
Cut off from the world,
they didn't care and the people came out

and walked together across the fields,
said they would always remember this time
and the lessons it had taught them.

Then the rains came and washed the snow away,
and the people soon forgot, and the town
became just another town, in just another place.

Idris Caffrey

To Distort the Bounds of Being

1

The lie is simple choice,
whichever path
through circumstance
my shadow travels,

as though I tread
but now the hollow fear
no pleasure can console
as long as direction resists.

And, absorbed by this,
nothing of each day
of my life will linger
to be, to remain forever;

nothing will survive
of the past to become
mine by name, by nature,
while the hours move on unseen.

2

The only truth in all this,
inasmuch as it is delusion,
forms, not balance, but doubt
to distort the bounds of being,

just as any sham embraced
draws on the measure of offence
no honesty can bleed from
the impression of trust I recall.

Within is my cosmos girdled,
teeming with anticipation
as to bluster laughter through
the imperturbable chill of day;

within, a once shrewd faith
contests my curiosity, over
and again, unwaveringly sane
in light of my confession of sin.

3

Alone, gone is my indifference
to past reflections, even if one
and the rest glint all around me –
for each belongs to me, still now,

along with the passion to resolve
the intimacy of solitary decline,
as when the quivering of my voice
defines the closeness of persuasion.

Lonely, all hereinafter is seeing
the vault of paradise as some higher
thought only thought when devotion
shimmers with gratitude for the dawn;

my invariable subsistence confirms
the warmth of another day without
sorrow to suckle at the breast of virtue,
draining the flaming spirit from the weak.

4

My scope of vision
encompasses the hinterland
only in kissing the earth will
I ever have the right to walk,

this land the night stained black
a wealth of uncompromising intuition
someone else made out of words
I hesitate, save none, to use to speak.

In sequence, from being
openly lost to descending
deep through throng and flood,
my cross I touch in acceptance;

of truth, I know never to dream
of motives as though of explanation,
for each reflects my circumstances
from first to finish, the season gone.

5

Not certain about the certain,
my space no further than the walls,
I adapt by way of the vanity of chance,
like the boy I know in images from memory,

and gain momentum, as though mindful
of death, speeding from dawn to dusk,
lingering only to till the soil of time
in a dream of unfolding absolution.

Splintered words come to promise me
my unseen, but perfect course through
the walls, through the stubbornly habitual
impenetrability of this foregone conclusion;

yet, the promise means little – insofar as
being no more than words, even though
sincere – for the lie is **my** simple choice,
never more than this.

John Mingay

Fat Bones and Water

'And the Lord shall guide thee continually, and satisfy thy soul
in drought and make fat thy bones: and thou shalt be like a
watered garden, and like a spring of water, whose waters fail
not.'

Isaiah 58.9, 11

Fat bones,
growth from the inside out,
not layers of fat laid down,
around
and under skin.

Marrow fat bones,
heart of life, of blood.
Lymphocytes,
white cells that fight
invasion and disease.

Fat bones and water,
protect us and give us life.
Clear cells and liquid,
soup-broth sustaining life.

Fat bones and water,
let us flourish and spill over.
Let there be more than enough.
Let us be more than enough.

Cath Nichols

Prayin f' Green

Ey, God mun, lissen up
t' what I gotta say
wen' t' the doctor's
sayz I gotta lump,
might not go away!

Maybe bard, maybe okay,
but wha ave I done
t' deserve it, eh?
I know I lied an urt,
know I sinned a bit,
but I never killed nobody,
never put myself
before my own famlee.

God mun, I tried didn I?
Done overtime till I
could ardly open my eyes,
t' buy em tidee books 'n' toys.
God mun, I done ower ouse up
summin lovely, my ands
signin ev'ry wall an ceilin.

Yew're the ol man I never ad
(mine never give a damn –
sorry 'bout-a language!).
I'm turnin t' yew now
f' my kids an missis
an, orright, I wanna be round
t' see Wales win-a Worl' Cup!

If yew got any clout at all
gimme a lump like a tip
that diggers cun scoop up,
cover over with a new skin,
so I become like ower Valley
in my prime o' green agen.

Mike Jenkins

Five Stones

My mother boiled for me a sheep's knee,
boiled it till steam filled the room
and froth bubbled round the pan,
the binding cartilage softened,
released five perfect knuckle bones.

I have them still, see here in my hand
polished with wear and my palm's sweat
each knob shining and grained like ivory.

Yes, they were used when I joined the guard,
to pass the time off duty, or to cast lots.
We quartered the Nazarene's garments,
but his coat was without seam,
woven from the top throughout,
too good to spoil. We took turns to throw.

I knew my knuckle bones were lucky.
Afterwards I vowed never again
to cast for gain, only for play.

Would you like to join me in a game?
Five Stones, Jacks, Round the World and Back.

Jane Shelton

Singular and Plural

No longer 'Thou',
reduced to 'You' –
the sacred cow
of being new –
I lost a relation,
the tender view,
that special affection,
the French 'tu'.

Language is
the thing that most
separates us

from fowl and beast,
and 'In the beginning
the Word' was true
and Thou was Thou
and you were you.

With plural God
I can agree –
inhabiting blood
and fire and sea –
but I want to honour,
childishly,
the singular
stupendous Thee.

Pat Buik

The Christmas Message

First prise apart the split ring
using a thumb nail,
allowing the security key
to thread into the steel circle.

This may only take a few seconds
or like me
a considerable number of years.

Once this certainty is in place,
peace of mind
is more likely to occur,
though there are still many circumstances
outside my control.

Perhaps the key
is not to believe in method alone,
just believe in my belief
that those restoring promises live today.
Also trust
my car doesn't get stolen.

Chris Antcliff

Before the Diagnosis

I don't know what's to come
But I do know that you're there.
I was curled up in your presence
Comfortable, sustained by prayer
On the operating table
In your smiling peace at rest
While the surgeon gave the injection
To perform the scheduled test.

In this morning's Bible reading
Stephen saw you standing there
At your Father's right hand, greeting
Welcoming, answering his prayer.

Christopher Payne

There Was a Place

There was a place
Where I took off my shoes
For the very holiness of it.
Holy ground, holy walls.
It was no bush which burnt:
It was my heart itself
Where music made a concert
Of thoughts, feelings, prayer,
Here, where the singers' hearts were silent
So the listeners' hearts might sing.
And if those doors are shut to me
They once were open.

Terence Handley MacMath

How Will It Come?

How will it come, the kiss of death?
This kiss of death, how will it come?
A butterfly lash upon the cheek
As light as a baby's breath?
The slow entwining limbs of a husband's
Inexorable embrace?
Or suddenly, though long expected,
Cold as Judas, on a human face?

Terence Handley MacMath

New Year

No east, no west.
Snow conceals the past.

The old year dreams
And the snow boy comes

With faith and light
To lead us gently out

Where we must go
Across the unmarked snow.

Susan Skinner

The Seed

Prayer is the seed.
Life is the field.
And God is the light.

Planted in the soul
Nurtured by grace
And sustained by patience.

Shrouded in mystery
Hidden in the depths
Yet primed to awaken.

Either to soar
To blossom and flourish
Or to wither and die.

Seed is the prayer.
The season is now.
And the potential is ours.

Neil Moran

Meaning

I would like to hear it in Spanish, whispered.
The words are not already in my head
so you could put them there, one by one.
I'll hear their sounds
and imagine what they mean.
I'll watch how your eyes move,
see how the light defines your face,
follow the rise and fall of your breath.

Don't translate and please
don't use these words again.
Throw them away.
I know what they mean.

Linda Chase

The Yes

Sometimes in my sleep I say yes,
the yes is more than I can say when I'm awake,
the yes is there neither in poetry nor prose,
it's as if my body says it knowing for my own sake
more than I think I know. In sleep yes,
then the shadowy memory of it, but faintly, yes.

David Hart

A Faith That Flies

I am in a prayer. I am in a word space.
Interludes of inspiration move me on. Towards
the dreams of today a future begins. What it is
to be left between ancient respect and the roar of
the unknown. I pick up the past like a lost infant,
adoring. This is perfect. But then I am changed by
curiosity, the fizz of the future, the claims of eternity.
I am within prayer. I join with the million.
I whisper what has to become. I fly between the sun
and the moon and ancient fables. What do they say?
What do I tell them? Between this prayer and
that perception I am aware of my wife watering
the summer season. And today the crows begin
to teach their young how to fly, to fly out,
discover, claim beyond. After half an hour
they journey out and find the nearest bough,
this thrust of universe. This prayer then,
compelled by our ancestors and ritual, released by
a faith that flies so far beyond.

David H. W. Grubb

A Quaker Silence

A Quaker silence has conviction in it
and it is held between reality and what
might be taken for mystery. Richard Crick
opens his soul to it each Sunday and has done
so for eighty years. Sara Rose always senses
a bell. She is eighteen. There is a bell in it
about to sound out a statement, a recognition;
it will happen one day. Meanwhile the Meeting
House resembles a tree. It smells of sky.
These small birds laying ideas
in nests of intuition.

David H. W. Grubb

Underdrawings

Renaissance art hidden for 500 years has been retrieved for the public view with computer technology.

I

These are the pictures we were not meant to see,
the outlines of pictures to be
hidden beneath oil and tempera,
invisible for five hundred years;
the dead Christ against a background of gold,
the figure of Mary Magdalene holding a vase;
Carlo Crivelli, for example, searching
for the perfect position for Christ's head;
figures and foregrounds changing
as Raphael and Bruegel get it right,
transcending the initial lines,
trusting light.

II

And with what words are we now attempting
to draft our lives, heart-whispers becoming
soul soliloquies, lives transforming on a page,
our determination to say what we have to say
against a background of rain;
these figures of parents and children and also strangers
and the holding of hands, hidden by distance
and discourse, finally getting it expressed between
the literary and the literal, the voices from orchards
and rooms and what we keep telling ourselves;
bells in the head, vocabularies of whispers
that underdraw all we mean, private carols
and secret sonnets, remembering vespers and
why we departed and the reason for prayers.

David H. W. Grubb

Spire

Had I ever seen a spire before,
had I ever understood?

In Ballymote, walking back from Ross's
rounding the corner, there it was
vaulting into the twilight summer sky—

sharpened
to its vanishing tip

that is God

at the stillest highest point
above the crown
(as of your head)

flanked by four small spire-lets
like candles, minor minarets

in-spired, then

where breathing in
and breathing out meet . . .
and to breathe is to be breathed

and then the whole building
the whole of the visible world
leaping to that point—

and yet staying, poised

earthed, anchored, tangible

in an ecstasy of darkening blue.

Jay Ramsay

Mary's Month

We thought it was winter
High up on the raw, windy ridge
Though diaries confirmed it was May –
Mary's month.
The time when the Christ-child
First stirred in the womb
Heralding Spring – new life within.

Imagine Mary – experiencing
Daily growth of body and mind,
Spirit-filled –
Pangs of joy
Leap in her heart
Mysteriously,
Saintly doubts dissolve,
Humble sincerity
Blossoms anew –
Mary's Springtime.

Here, amid weeping bluebells,
Soaked by fresh rain;
The treasured magnolia dying again,
We thought it was Winter
High on the ridge
At Holmhurst St Mary.

As silence fell,
Truth was revealed
Today, every day
Spring moves toward Summer
When we stay close to Jesus
Like Mary did.

Seeds of contentment are nurtured,
Mirrored here, high on the ridge,
In the dank, misty garden
One solitary wisteria bud
Waiting to bloom.

Each palest petal
Perfectly formed
Anticipates warmth
From the hidden sun.
Every branch will burst anew,
Promised sequel to Easter,
Signalling Summer –
Healing and Wholeness
Barely begun.

Wendy Whitehead

As Above So Below

blades of grass singly	water falling
feel the water table	white order
blue of old time	water of rain
feel the order	white space
find its level	water of ocean
secret life	space is order
	azure water sky water
	feel the light
	squeaking through
	white curtains

blades of grass singly

plant life vegetating

feel the water table

juice rising to meet

blue of old time

the pink canvas hints below

feel the order

the juice rising to its level

find its level

plants are fed with juices

secret life

secret life vegetating below earth

water falling

white order

water of rain

white space

water of ocean

space is order

azure water sky water

feel the light

deep blue of evening

squeaking through

the moment when light

white curtains

when light is twilight

order is not order
it is only the appearance of order
order is illusion there is no order
move closer into the painting
grain of canvas
soft edges of paint appear as order
there is no order

Angela Topping
in response to a painting by Rupert M. Loydell

DISCOVERING
FAITH
THROUGH Points
of Light

Points of Light

The desire to create a special space in which to contemplate, approach and communicate with God pertains to many cultures and many faiths. We carry this place in our heads and in our hearts, of course, but the need is for something more visible, an actual space dedicated and blessed and more than an enabling symbol of what we wish to signal and say and pray.

These spaces may be in the form of pavilions, rooms, gardens, sanctuaries, retreats, lodges, shrines, altars, enclaves or circles, and in Christian experience and expression the garden has been important for centuries as a symbol or theme or location.

Whatever forms are chosen and whatever symbols and images and artefacts are employed, common to many of them are simple forms and natural elements. Whenever chapels, churches and cathedrals create the space for communal worship and celebration, individual meditation and tranquillity are needed and places where – for a while – we can leave the ordinary and day to day and enter another place.

Wood, stone and water comprise what appear to be basic elements and a point of light.

The point of light may be natural and embrace the place as a whole or a focus, the light entering in one specific place or series of entrances. The eye and the mind are drawn to it from a position of secluding darkness.

The point of light might be crystals, glass, candle, a space between stones which is an opening to energy, a well, a view of sun or moon or sky. A stained-glass window. A crucifix. A bell. A drum.

The point of light can be physical or in the mind. A dance. Music. A poem. A short story. A letter. A conversation.

The point of light is also created when something is discovered between the individual and the place that draws us to God. The moment of truth. The revelation. Seeing the eyes of Jesus and the mind of God.

A large number of Polish workers came to the South Wales valleys after the Second World War, but in our town they didn't form a distinct community and there were no Polish churches or clubs. The Poles were gentle, hard-working men who were absorbed into Valley life, many of them marrying Welsh girls.

The Wife's Story

He just appeared at the hospital one day, asking for work. It was autumn, a year after the war. The gardener gave him a trial run. He was a good worker, so he stayed. The first time I saw him, he was sweeping the path leading up to the kitchen, holding the broom in one hand, just like in that photograph. The other arm hung loose at his side and I remember wondering if he'd broken it and not got it set properly. He brushed the leaves off the steps for me so I wouldn't slip. Then, he smiled shyly and sort of bowed. He couldn't have been any more than seventeen.

He didn't tell us much about himself. Just that his name was Josef, he came from Poland and he spoke 'no good English'. We were used to Polish men turning up in our town, looking for jobs down the pit or in the steelworks. Hard-working and quiet they were, never causing any bother. One of the girls working with me in the hospital kitchen said she heard Josef had tried the pit but when he had gone into the cage and the old colliers had dropped it like a stone, the way they always do to scare the new boys, he'd gone hysterical. Brought up screaming and shouting, like a madman, she said. But Cook, who had a soft spot for Josef by then, said you couldn't believe all you heard in the pub and Jane was no better than she should be going to the 'Ty Mawr' anyway. And that put an end to that.

Josef always worked outside in the gardens. He couldn't be persuaded to do any jobs inside the hospital even in the wettest weather. His gentle manner made him a favourite with all the staff, though he seldom spoke. The nurses made a pet of him, bringing him clothes, although they were still on the ration, but he always returned to his baggy corduroy trousers, held up with string, and the faded check shirt, six sizes too big. Cook was determined to fatten him up but he refused to come into the kitchen. So, I started to take his dinner out to the veranda. He was always grateful and soon he was bringing me little presents. Useless bits and pieces, really; a handful of blackberries, a pretty feather, leaving them for me to find when I went back to collect his dishes. I tried to teach him English. I used to point things out and tell him the words. He loved it when I told him the names of flowers and he would try to repeat their names, rolling the soft words in his mouth as if they were jelly-babies. Morning glory, love-lies-bleeding, burning bush. I took in some of my father's old seed catalogues to help our lessons along. He laughed out loud when I explained that my name, Eirlys, was Welsh for snowdrop, pointed at me and said 'girl, not flower'. But in January he found the very first snowdrops and left them for me by his empty plate. I still have them, pressed between tissue paper in my Bible.

And that's how things were until that nosey old Matron went poking around the outhouses. But anyway, she found out Josef was sleeping down there, behind one of the sheds. He'd made himself a sort of nest. Branches woven around an old bed-frame and covered in scraps of cloth and leaves. No one had realised. Well, Matron just wanted to sack him on the spot, but we all rallied round. I was really scared of Matron, but I spoke up and said if I could run home and speak to Mam, she would probably let Josef stay in our spare room. She'd been talking about taking a lodger now we knew for definite my brother wouldn't be coming back from the war.

Well then, that's how Josef moved in with us. He was no bother. He used to give his pay packet straight to Mam to take his keep and then she used to dole out the rest to him from a special jam jar on the dresser, like pocket money. She started to fuss over him and Dad was pleased because it eased her grief over my brother's death. She even gave him a pair of Gwyn's shoes.

I knew, though, that something was troubling Josef. I used to stay awake at night, listening to him moaning. Pitiful, it was, like a snared bird. One night, I couldn't stand it any longer. I crept into his room, slipped into bed beside him and held him tight, soothing him like a baby until he was peaceful. He felt so fragile, bones as light as a sparrow's and his poor dislocated arm was like a broken wing. I was soon tiptoeing in every night, taking care to be back in my own bed before morning. We were total innocents. Sometimes I felt I was a mother, comforting a child terrified by a nightmare. At others, it felt as if my brother was still alive and we were little again. Of course, one Sunday, I didn't wake up in time and my father found us curled up together in the narrow bed. There was a row and within a month we were standing outside the Chapel, covered in confetti. We look like two frightened children in our wedding photograph, caught out trying on the grown-ups' clothes.

And like children, we carried on listening to my father. Dad started to put the pressure on Josef, insisting he gave up gardening at the hospital and find a job with tidy money so we could save up for our own home. Being a bit of a boss down the steelworks, Dad used his influence and before long, Josef was working there. But it was hopeless. He just couldn't concentrate shut indoors and was a danger to the other men. Soon he was just sweeping floors. Naturally, his wages were cropped, so Dad made him look for extra work on his days off, odd jobs for other people, chopping sticks, that sort of thing.

Now, here's the bit I find really hard to talk about, when it all started to go wrong. One afternoon, Josef was down the Manse, helping prune the fruit trees. Mrs Evans, the Minister's wife, came banging on our door shouting and screaming. 'He's running up my phone bill. He's telephoning his mother in Poland!' I ran down the street as if the hounds of hell were at my heels. I found Josef in Mrs Evans' parlour, cradling the telephone to his ear. I took it from him, but when I listened, there was no one there, just a crackling noise. 'Have you been speaking to your mother, Josef?' I asked gently. He shook his head sadly, 'No. Not Mother. Angels.'

After that, he just seemed to crumble away. His whole being seemed even less solid somehow. He was afraid of his reflection and I had to cover the mirror in our bedroom with an old sheet. He even said there were faces in the puddles in the street screaming at him. We often found him wandering up on the mountain, or picking up litter in the park, regardless of the weather. And he would knock on the doors of the Big Houses, asking to use the telephone. I tried to find out what was troubling him. He seemed to be looking for someone, but I don't know who. He never talked about his family and I wondered what had happened to them. I knew about the camps in Poland, had seen them on the newsreels in the pictures. I asked if he had been a prisoner, or made to work in a camp, but he pretended he didn't understand, although I knew his English was good enough. All he would tell me was the Voices wanted him again. This frightened me and I started to cry. He took my hand. 'Maybe angels,' he said, hopefully, and I was even more confused.

Then, one day, he just didn't come home from work. I walked miles, looking for him, but no luck, so my father went down the pub to speak to the men on Josef's shift. They told him some Polish boys had turned up – looking for work – and Josef had been talking to them. He'd become very agitated but they had been speaking in Polish and the only word they had understood was 'Wolverhampton'.

A month later, Josef still hadn't come home. Dad made a few enquiries and went up to Wolverhampton himself. I don't know what he found. 'You can forget that damned foreigner, my girl. He's not coming back,' was all he said to me. And he was right. This photograph is the first time I have set eyes on Josef for over fifty years. He's not my husband now, of course. The divorce came through years ago. I waited, hoping he would come back, but Daddy had no peace of mind while I was neither one thing nor the other. So, I let him sort out all of the paperwork for me but I never remarried.

I knew it was Josef, right away, just by the way he's standing, exactly the same as the first time I saw him, sweeping the hospital steps, holding the brush like a crutch. Josef has been in my thoughts a lot recently, so I'm not surprised about this newspaper article turning up. I'm not shocked either. It sounds hard, but I'm glad he's living outside. And I'm glad the Council have the sense to see that they would kill him if they put him in a home. You see, I think I finally understand him. A preacher came to our Chapel a few weeks ago. He had been working in Russia as a missionary and he told us about the tradition they have there of 'holy fools'. People we'd call a bit simple, but are, I don't quite know how to put it, 'touched by God', I think he said. The people there respect them for their holiness and innocence and I think Josef was a bit like that. We can't see it clearly, but the Asians in Wolverhampton can. I always wondered if he'd been damaged by something that happened in the war and maybe he had, but now I think it was more than that, something that was always inside him. Something spiritual. Perhaps what Josef was looking for was God. And I hope he found Him. 'Fools for Christ's sake,' the missionary said, and Russia isn't so very far from Poland, is it?

Sandra Buttrick

The Relay

Talk had been of little else for the last two weeks of term. In every part of the schoolyard boys gathered in huddles to lay bets, brag about whom they knew would win and generally discuss the strategies of the teams. Their white shirts nonchalantly hanging out of their trousers and their burgundy-and-black ties loosely hanging from their collars, as if the effort of pushing them up that extra inch would somehow render the owner uncool. By the afternoon the excitement was palpable, and as the final bell announced the start of the summer holidays it felt as if the lid had finally been released on a hothouse of anticipation.

Our school was set at the top of a hill and as the shrill noise split open the harmony of the countryside it resembled the turning on of a tap, with children appearing from all corners of every school building, each descending at varying speeds down the slope towards the river.

I had longed to be selected as part of my House team and when finally I was asked to join this elite group I felt as if I had suddenly been awarded fins and gills, which would surely help me in my dash across the river. For that was the competition: each of the three Houses elected three swimmers to swim, in relay, across the river and back.

I waited nervously in the changing rooms with the rest of my team, taking a moment to gather my thoughts.

'All right, Matt? Let's go kick some butt.' Mark slapped me hard on the shoulder and together with Luke we put on our trunks and tracksuits and opened the door to where our destiny awaited.

'Have you seen Jon's new bike? Wicked!' Luke said enthusiastically as we left the school gates behind us.

'Yeah,' I replied with envy.

'I'd love a bike like that,' Luke sighed, 'but my dad would never buy me one. I know, maybe I could get a paper round and save up!'

'You'd have to work for the next ten years to save up enough for that bike . . . you dopey baggage,' Mark chipped in, pushing Luke playfully off the pavement.

'That's right, put the dampers on it . . . I can dream, can't I?' Luke responded, pretending to sulk.

I looked over at Mark's raven-black hair as it glinted in the sunlight, slightly damp around the temples in response to the warmth of the day. He was an exceptional athlete, Head of House and beyond doubt the most popular boy at school. But through all this he still retained a friendliness, a normality, seemingly quite unaware of the effect that he had on all those around him. We would do anything for Mark; such was his star quality.

Luke appeared the very antithesis of Mark. A frail-looking, ginger-haired boy whose skin was so freckled that I was sure one day the freckles might all join together and instead of his usual deathly pallor he would instantly sport a sun-kissed Mediterranean tan. Funny how this never happened. However, despite his appearance, once in the water Luke transformed into the most graceful swimmer I had ever seen. His technique, style and ease made him a truly magnificent sight. Luke was born to swim, and I often felt sorry that he could not be in the water all the time, it was where he belonged.

And then there was me, Matt, a good all-rounder who was guaranteed to give one hundred percent when the time came, but who somehow lacked the grace and finesse of the other two. Still, I was happy to have made the team and could only do my best, I told myself.

And there we were, three friends joined together in our quest to succeed; three friends prepared to put ourselves on the line for each other; three friends forever united by our shared experience.

It was the noise of the cheering that brought my mind back to the present, and we immediately stopped our easy banter to survey the scene. Boys were crowding the banks of the river; some had abandoned their shoes and socks to stand in the murky waters, thus ensuring a ringside view. Others had opted to watch from further back where the natural slope of the ground elevated them above the crowds in front. But all of them were shouting for their House, all of them hoping that the noise would somehow lift and inspire their friends to victory.

I suddenly realised how nervous I had become and that my heart was now pounding as a drum heralding the commencing battle. I blew out a few sharp breaths, and turned to my friends. They had already stripped off their tracksuits and were calmly smiling at faces in the crowd. I looked over to the other teams and managed to lock eye contact with a couple of boys I knew well. We nodded at each other as if to say 'good luck, but be prepared for a hard fight'.

And suddenly we were being called to take our positions. We had decided that Luke would swim first, then me and finally Mark. We had all watched this event many times as we had worked our way up the school, and had discussed the safest places to dive in, the right line to take to keep out of the strongest currents and where to turn for the return leg. Nothing had gone unexplored or undiscussed.

'On yer marks . . . set . . . go.' Luke's lithe body emerged from under the water as he surfaced from his dive; within seconds he had reached the other side and turned for his sprint back to hand over to me. I glanced over at the other two swimmers and realised that we were marginally in the lead. I felt sick to my stomach, as I knew it was only moments before I too had to perform. And suddenly I had dived into the greeny-brown depths. The iciness of the water momentarily shocked my system, but only for an instant as I surfaced and quickly got into my stroke. I tried to focus all thoughts on increasing the speed of my leg-kick and allowing my arms to cut cleanly through the water. And as I made my turn I realised that we were all in a line, neck and neck, nothing between us. And so I handed over to Mark, and somehow we had known that it would be left up to him. The scene was set for him to be the victorious one. I had done enough and he would win, as he had always done, as had been his destiny since birth.

I watched him dive over the top of me, his regal body casting a shadow as it blocked out the sun and I turned away, breathing hard, exhausted from the exertion of my swim. But as I stood in the water I gradually became aware of a growing hush among the crowd, and instinctively I knew that something was wrong.

I looked behind me and saw only two swimmers, where three should have been. Mark's familiar form was nowhere to be seen.

The other two swimmers had now reached the bank and were on the return leg, their bodies surging through the pristine surface of the water. I was aware of Luke diving into the river, shrieking 'Where is he?' and I joined my friend in our search, still not fully comprehending the situation.

The two remaining boys had now finished the race, but I had not seen who had won, and still Mark did not appear. All the other swimmers were now in the water bobbing under the surface, as a sickly panic rose in my throat and I too sunk beneath the murky depths.

It was someone else who managed to bring him up from the riverbed. A heavy weight, all crumpled over. His long limbs hanging limply, lifeless like a stone, as with great effort we helped to carry him to the riverbank. There was utter silence, as he lay motionless, peaceful, asleep. Moments passed and no one moved, all locked with fear. All eyes fixed on the painfully still body, and only the river maintained its constant flow. The gurgling, spiralling water moving downstream, taking all things to their natural conclusion.

It was at that moment that I turned and observed a small

boy walk from the back of the crowd. With slow purposeful steps he carved a direct route to where Mark lay and bent over my dear friend.

There was at once something familiar and reassuring about him, but I was positive that I had never seen him before. He quietly knelt down next to the sculpted figure, which had moments before been so full of vitality and life, and cupped its beautiful chin in his small hands. He then bent down and touched Mark's lips as if in a kiss and for a fleeting moment there appeared to be a radiance that transcended that briefest of exchanges. A tenderness, a kindness, a love.

The little boy lifted his head, and I was struck by the innocence of his face, the compassion, and the truth behind his pale blue eyes, and I looked down at my friend. And as I watched I saw him suddenly fill with life as he took a long breath and opened his eyes.

'Get up, Mark,' the little boy whispered as he helped him to his feet.

Then everything went mad. There were boys jumping down onto the riverbank, hugging Mark, and lifting him onto their shoulders, whoops of delight for our friend who had returned to us, for Mark the hero, for Mark the champion.

And through all of this I looked over at the small boy who had now fallen to the back of the crowd and was turning to walk away, and I realised that I did know him, I had always known him, and so do you.

Fiona Dowthwaite

Prayer and Laughter?

Out of his generous initiative and unfathomable invention, God sends us gifts for prayer that are as surprising as they are diverse. The gift of Tongues is perhaps the best recognised; some are given the gift of Stillness, and others the gift of Tears (particularly well documented by the Eastern Orthodox Church). Perhaps less well known is the gift of Laughter. Among the many touchings and anointings given by the Holy

Spirit in the privacy of personal prayer, this last is among the most releasing and confirming.

For centuries, since the put-down by clerics of the popular Feast of Fools in the Middle Ages, laughter has been frowned upon in church. Times, thank God, are changing, and congregations are becoming more attractive to newcomers by the ease with which laughter ripples through them. Laughter itself is a powerful force: it binds people together, it lifts low spirits, it raises optimism, it increases the level of oxygen to every cell in the body, it strengthens the immune system, it increases the production of endorphins, it has a high 'feel good' factor! That is, if the laughter is shared and inclusive: of course, there are plenty of incidents of snide, derogatory and sneering laughter – for that sort the Bible uses the word 'scorn', and we also should use a totally separate name for it.

These days there is a considerable bibliography on the theological aspects of laughter, and much discussion around if, when and how Jesus laughed (some of this is covered in my book **Come, Let Us Play**). In this short piece I'd like to offer ideas on the gift of laughter in private prayer.

First, let me tell you a story of something that happened to me. It was around the time I was doing some research on the benefits of laughter in the relief of stress. A 'laughter workshop' was advertised as taking place in London, and I duly went. The presenter had hired one of the large guildhalls in the city, and was expecting around four hundred people to attend. Four of us turned up – that was a joke right at the start! The presenter generously agreed to continue with the programme, and we spent an hour or two building up confidence between us, doing various stretching exercises, and learning some background theory. Significantly, none of this included anything to do with wisecracks or punchlines or comic acts – it was just about the experience of laughter itself. Then we were pointed to large piles of mattresses and sleeping bags arranged around the hall and invited to use as many as we liked to build our own personal nest. This we did, and when we were thoroughly comfortable we were led into a deeply relaxed space of peace.

Into this still and peaceful place we were invited by our

leader to bring our five most pressing problems. It seemed an odd thing to do, but we were a compliant group and we silently took our worst pains and worries into the centre of ourselves. 'Stay there with the pain', we were told, until we felt a grumble (of anger? of rebellion? of dismay?) 'in the deepest part of your body, at the base of your belly.'

'Let the grumble turn into a rumble', we were told, 'as it starts to rise.'

'Let the rumble turn into a gurgle . . . and the gurgle into a chuckle. Let it come, let it rise, don't hold it back, don't let it stop . . .'

'The chuckle will turn into a laugh . . .' we were told; and it did.

And the laugh grew and grew until it was almost uncontainable. We were holding our sides, rolling in our sleeping bags. We weren't laughing **at** anything, but **with** – it felt to me as if it was with the cosmos; the pain of our ribs shaking was almost unbearable. We laughed and laughed: nothing hysterical, mind you, but such laughter!

After about ten minutes we were told we only had one minute left, which set us off again, but when the minute closed and we were told to stop, we did, almost instantly. Then we went back into our still, peaceful place. The leader asked us to look again at our problems, and at what had happened to them.

Do you think they had gone? Disappeared? No . . . but every one of them had changed shape. It was as if we had been reassured that God, also, was handling them, juggling with them as he juggles with the planets, and he would stay with them until they had been resolved. **We** were in it together, and the lightening of the load still lives with me.

But what, I think I hear you saying, has all this to do with prayer? It's so difficult to put explicitly into words. But sometimes, some precious times, when someone is bowed down with concern in their praying, there will be sent a rumble at the base of the belly ('belly' is a fine scriptural word, laden with meaning, which is used from Genesis to Revelation in the Greek, but which for our polite modern ears has been expunged and changed into terms such as 'inner feelings' or 'deep resources'). If it is unhindered it will grow, and rise and gurgle until it becomes full-blown, care-freed laughter. The sort of laughter Jesus would have shared after a day's hard fishing with his disciples, over a barbecued supper. It won't be laughter **at** anything, but it's a laughter that joins in with the optimism of the new creation. It is undoubtedly God's gift.

Talking about it may be difficult, and I am finding writing about it even more so. But whenever it comes up I find people who say, 'I know about that! I know what you're talking about! But I haven't told anyone because I thought it was only me, and perhaps I shouldn't.' And people have shared their stories with me. That's why I've had the temerity to share this with you.

If, at any time, you feel this about to happen to you, that the Spirit is offering you a chance to let go into his release and his freedom, don't ever squash it down out of inhibition. It is a lavishing of grace not to be resisted. Praise God.

Wanda Nash

Praying and Playing

This is a piece for readers who are open and prepared for different insights: insights that are as old as the hills and the trees that clapped their hands (Isaiah 55.12) and the streets of Jerusalem being filled with boys and girls playing (Zechariah 8.5).

Just take a minute or two to sit back and imagine you are with a child who is special to you. Any age, either sex, any place. Think about the ways in which you bond together, and what you yourself enjoy most being in the company of this child.

Now, prepare yourself for the picture of that special child approaching you solemnly, head bowed, self-blaming and penitential, pleading. What would it feel like if that was the usual, even habitual, way the child came towards you? Mightn't you feel there was a whopping gap somewhere in the relationship between you both?

If that picture is uncomfortable, take a minute to name what means most to you as you interact with a special child. Is it when you are teaching them, showing them how to do something? Is it praying with them? Or feeding them? Or is the greatest delight of all when you are playing with them?

Now, to be a bit fanciful, look at those two words again – praying and playing. The only difference between them is the shape of the second letter. In the first word, the figure 'r' is bending over and half hiding; in the second word, the figure 'l' is standing upright and grounded, steadily waiting for anything that might happen, freed up to welcome it. The fanciful bit is to relate this difference to the ways we have thought about prayer down the centuries – the first as it is absorbed by the person in the pew, the other as taught by the mystics.

Jesus described God as 'Father'. He prayed to his Father using the word 'Abba' – the nearest equivalent word we have is 'Dad'. Can we, ourselves, hope to approach the God who is our Father with that real, spontaneous delight of dad and daughter, or dad and son?

Again and again in the Gospels Jesus is recorded as urging us to be like children. So much so that he said '**unless** you become like a child you will **never** enter the kingdom of God'.

While we puzzle out the significance of this strange injunction (surely we also have to be mature, responsible, accountable, competent, knowledgeable and in-the-right?) it is useful to distinguish 'childish' qualities – those that St Paul said we must leave behind – from 'childlike' qualities – those that Jesus recommends to us. Often people identify 'childishness' as something about being sulky and obstinate, throwing tantrums, constantly wanting one's own way, telling lies and cheating, ganging up to thwart adults, contriving attention or being secretive and self-centred. By contrast, 'childlikeness' brings up words such as trust and spontaneity, adventure and curiosity, full of fun yet enjoying tenderness and intimacy and wonder; it is about being vulnerable, but somehow also abandoned.

In the thirteenth century, St Mechtild of Magdeburg, one of the group of Rhine mystics, declared 'God wants me (**me**!?) as his playmate'. I'd like to tell you about a group to whom I suggested that they list the characteristics they would choose in an ideal playmate. Among the group was a young, middle-aged couple who had remained silent and distant all morning, sitting together holding hands on a settee at the side of the room. I shall call them Sam and Jean. After a few minutes of discussion this is the list that the group suggested:

As a child looking for a best playmate, I would look for someone who

- won't boss me around
- accepts me even when I sometimes drop the ball
- shares adventures with me
- is available, just there, at any time
- won't rat on me
- likes doing the same sorts of things I like doing
- isn't out to hurt me
- I can be silly with, who laughs with me but not at me
- is just there, sitting with me, without needing to talk
- is loyal and together and backs me up
- listens, though sometimes we never stop talking

At that stage Sam jumped up and exclaimed, 'When you have had a real personal tragedy, **that's what God is like**.' For me, that turned into one of the most defining moments of my spiritual life. Sam and Jean had just lost their thirteen-year-old daughter from cancer.

Play and prayer are both about relationship. Playfulness is about abandoning my own concerns into the inventiveness and unexpectedness of the other. It is the ultimate let-go. When I play I let go of my need to strive hard, to prove and justify myself; it is a letting go of my worries and anxieties; letting go of my childishness, my look-at-me-ness, my not-getting-what-I-want-ness; I let go of my self-pity and that relentless tirade of self-criticism; I can even let go of my need for approval – for a while! As Richard Holloway has put it, 'the real faith of a Christian is more like a rolling jazz session than a march on the barrack square' (**Dancing on the Edge**, 1997, Fount Paperbacks, p. 200).

So how do we actually **do** it, or at least begin to do it? Different people will have different methods, but this is one suggestion that has been well tested. It's about using your own imagination to form a picture, and then just watching what happens, without any deliberate interference.

First of all, get into a place of deep, peaceful relaxation. Then watch while you are a child again: not necessarily the child you actually were, but the child you would have liked to have been. You are playing on your own, contentedly, warm and safe. Watch where you are; what you are doing; your body language; your feelings.

Maybe you can imagine Jesus as a child too. Will the child Jesus want to come and join in your play? Or does he, in your imagination, stay apart, aloof, too 'different' to be played with? Who invites whom to join them . . .? Which of you welcomes the other . . .? What happens next . . .? How does that feel?

When the time comes for Jesus to leave, he tells you he will be around again soon. So watch as you say a temporary goodbye to each other, and then see yourself back to a place where you are safe and loved. And take time to give thanks for whatever has been shown to you.

▲▲▲▲▲▲

Perhaps you might like to imagine Jesus in his adult ministry. He sees you playing on your own as a child. Does he come straight in and invade your personal space? How do you make contact with each other . . .? (Do you want to make contact?) Watch your body language and his . . . What happens next . . .? Try to name how you feel. After a while you might like to ask him how he prays to his Father, and to show you how to do it. Maybe there will be a recognition in you of the delight and mutuality and excitement he shows when he is talking to God. Maybe it can be mirrored in your prayer, sometimes, too.

When the time comes for Jesus to leave, he tells you he will be around again soon. So watch as you say a temporary goodbye to each other, and then see yourself back to a place where you are safe and loved. And take time to give thanks for whatever has been shown to you.

Playing and praying. Such a natural juxtaposition. Sometimes it dances and leaps like the flame of the Holy Spirit; sometimes

it is like playing hide-and-seek with the Father – as described in 'The Cloud of Unknowing'. Sometimes it is simply sitting still with Jesus, making daisy chains on the Mount of Olives. Sometimes it can heal hurting childhood memories, sometimes it can melt frozen adult hearts. Each time you do it, you'll be shown something different. Its surprises lie in the lightening up of my grown-upness; the joying with creation as it claps its hands; and the growing realisation of the love of our Father, as he shares it with his children, his own sons and daughters.

Wanda Nash

Reflections

All around us reflections change the world. The early sun turns grass into blades of white glass, puddles turn fields into skies. At night the invisible sun reflects worlds from billions of miles away and gives us the changing moon. All of nature reflects the turning of the world, the inevitable seasons of growth, maturity and decay. And though we are part of this marvellous universe we often forget it in the business of our lives. Yet in deep quiet we find that even the smallest thing reflects ourselves. Even a minute and insignificant raindrop is part of us. Its fragility, translucence, silence, shadow, impermanence, reflect qualities that are in ourselves and through it we become aware of the unity of creation.

Susan Skinner

Peculiar Navigation

A Prose Meditation

Stepping to the lectern is to enter a circumscribed space: the shadow of responsibility chalked out, Prospero-like, around my words. Heightened awareness descends, akin to being on-stage. I become acutely aware of coughs, shuffles, eyes flickering. At the same time, a microphone lends distance and will give the voice a strange, impersonal objectivity.

The first problem is the text: what was straightforwardly logical when drafted suddenly seems to present opportunities for improvisation. Riffs, thoughts, swarm just beyond the grasp, near the ancient rafters. Resist? Indulge? It is a temptation and therefore must be weighed in the balance. In the end, some form of retracing steps or re-enactment must take place. This often makes the prayers seem second-hand to the reader: the rehearsal, alone, was the original prayer. No one else is aware of this staleness, this strange weightlessness.

Balance: shift from foot to foot. Place the hands carefully. Remind yourself that this is not teaching, nor lecturing of any sort. A whole tonal range is unavailable: there is nothing pedagogic about this encounter, just a peculiar navigation to be made, poling our way through the silent darkness. The coins of silence weigh heavily on our eyelids. Now we are listening and something very close is listening to us: step up and begin.

Martin Caseley

Sequence

Each night, Tony takes his lower legs off and leaves them in the hall, his jeans fallen down around the plastic feet. And he climbs into his loft and lies beside his dear, bowlegged wife who has beautiful handwriting (I know because she writes me) and he falls asleep to the sounds of Uptown Chicago: shots fired, sirens, screaming and yelling, talking and laughing, doors opening, doors closing, and basically people just moving about. And each night, Tony dreams of flying. His legs are never there; he has no feet of his own. But he's rising into the Irish air and coasting above the hills. Over those trees and streams and rivers and rooftops. Over those British Isle cathedrals, barely missing the spires, and watching the churchgoers coming and going and seeing his family among the crowd. He glides like an albatross to the grave where his little appendages were given a proper Catholic burial thirty-five years earlier. And then he feels whole again.

I slept on my father's grave tonight. It's the only place I could find some peace. And of course I dreamt about him as I lay there with him, and of course he spoke to me as if I were a child, telling me over and over that everything would be alright. Then I woke up staring at the still blue sky, knowing everything was not alright, feeling like it never will be, and hanging onto the earth so my body wouldn't float away against my will. I was grasping my father's grave, holding fast to my life, watching the world above me, and twice thought a waving American flag was someone walking toward me.

Just like my grandmother kept the Christmas tree up in the living room until Easter, waiting for my father to come home from the war, I keep this plastic wristband on, waiting for her to come back into my life. She didn't send me to the psych ward but she wasn't there when I got out, either. We spoke on the phone on my second day there and I slept that night in paper pajamas, dreaming of a visit which hasn't happened yet. Father forgive us all.

The night is nearly over; the day is almost here. I see the grey light through the slats of my blinds, so I know it's that time. But the fear which was grabbing me just a few days back has not begun to grab again. I lie on soft sheets, listening for the birds, waiting for those old feelings from the known and unknown to stir, overtake my mind, strangle my heart, hold on tight and not let go. I listen for the birds, and I listen closely for the sound of my own breathing, to tell me if I made it through the darkness. Somebody once told me that the old man dies a slow death, and habits formed over the years are so difficult to break. And it seems to me that joy, even when it comes in the form of emptiness, is a thing which will surely take some getting used to; it's a way of living I've never known anything of, it's a way to stand up, and look and not just listen.

Bruce Bitmead

Searching

One day, a young man set out to find God. He listened to a number of very well-respected authorities, and, when he wasn't working to support himself, he either read what other people had written about God, or volunteered to help less fortunate people than himself: and gradually he learnt more and more about the nature of God: but he still couldn't find Him.

In the course of his wanderings, after many years, the now elderly man eventually came to a silent, bare place where there was no one to question, nothing to read, nothing useful to do . . . and he realised that, in his mind and consciousness, God was already a reality. He was finally sure that he knew as much about God as he needed to know to be sure of His existence. He hadn't found God: rather, at last, he had let God find him. And he turned to go home with a huge new peacefulness.

> God, when I know you do not exist,
>   Help me to ask the alternative question –
>   If you did exist,
> How would you want me to live and behave
>   So that I might give you a chance to find me?

R. G. Ferguson

My Father Had a Field

My Father had a field. He worked the earth and he fed it. He had a purpose for this field. It was to yield the bread of life. He had a seed so big and ripe he'd never had one like it. He loved to hold it in his hand and contemplate its fruitfulness. Then one day he planted the seed. He was sad to let it go, but he knew it would yield well and as he watered and he watched, it grew up strong and green. As the seasons passed, it yielded as he had hoped. He cut it down, he threshed it hard, he winnowed it and tossed it. His seed had gone, but in its place twelve more were in his hand. He planted them in his fertile field and they also yielded well. They too were cut and threshed and tossed and his harvest gathered in. And so it happened time and time again, the yield increasing yearly and all the time my father held in mind the purpose of the field. At last he gathered in enough to take a sack for milling and all his precious seed he poured between the granite stones. He watched them turn and grind the seed. He watched the flour spill from the husk. His heart was full, a mixture of dread and exultation. He knew it would not be long. He took the flour, only a small bag but enough to make the bread he was waiting for. He prepared the flour for the dough. He sifted it, not just once but several times, each time with a smaller mesh. He wanted the finest flour for his bread. At last all was ready. But first he climbed a high mountain to a spring where the water was most fresh and pure and sweet. He collected enough in a golden cup and carefully carried it down to the valley. Then he poured the water out and mixed it with the bread flour. He kneaded the dough and shaped it into a pattern well known, then placed it deep inside the oven. The fire inside was all that was needed to complete the act. Finally the hour had come and the bread was ready. His heart was full again, but this time with joy and exultation for his planned purpose was to be fulfilled. He took the bread in his hands, then he broke it and as he did so his heart cried out, 'It is finished'.

E. Charlotte Wright

The Travellers

Some travellers, as they journeyed, found themselves travelling through the night. It was very dark and all they had to light their way was a candle each, which they held close to them for fear that the night winds would blow them out. Then at the darkest hour, shortly before dawn, they came to a last corner which appeared the most threatening and dangerous of all.

It was then that they understood something remarkable. With each step of their dark journey, their meagre, flickering candles – which they held so close and which threw such a feeble light – were being changed. As they had gone forward with each draught of chill night air and each flicker of flame, the candles were being transformed into diamonds – strong, resilient, magnificent diamonds.

They marvelled as they thought of how these gems would catch the full radiance of the coming dawn, projecting cascades of colour and beauty on all around. They knew then that their light would no longer be from candles held close and safe lest the flames be snuffed. They knew instead that as they held these precious and magnificent jewels up, away from themselves, they would catch all the light they needed and more.

Then, with the mystery of inner sight, the travellers saw jewels within themselves and they journeyed on into the new day.

E. Charlotte Wright

Letter to God

Dear God,

I am writing You this letter because I cannot pray.

Oh I can chant the responses all right, but that's not really me praying to You, is it? I have tried. I've even joined a home group. Boy, they could pray for England. They would win an award if there was one going. They are an interesting bunch. Some are young, some old, all are very kind and welcoming. They all seem very enthusiastic about You and can quote from the Bible. The only quote I can remember is 'Jesus wept'. I guess that is because it's the shortest verse in the New Testament. They flick through their Bibles looking for the passages with relish. I am always way behind (I still can't find 1 John – I have to look it up in the index). Anyway, at the end of our home group meetings, we pray. Well, they pray. I just keep my head bowed, my eyes shut, and hope they don't ask me to say anything. They launch into praying with gusto: praying for those of us in the home group; praying for personal problems; praying for South Africa; praying for the government (huh, they need praying for); praying for world peace. You should hear some of them. Hey, I guess You do, so you'll know what I mean. Meanwhile I sit all quiet, listening to all of this, unable to speak. They always leave a pause at the end, a pregnant pause, an expectant pause and, you know what it's like, if there is a loud silence you always feel as if someone should fill it. Some folk have another go and say another prayer. I feel they are waiting for me to say something. I say nothing. My mind is blank, my heart is closed and I cannot pray.

I've tried praying to You at night, before I go to bed, just like a little child, like you see on those sickly twee Christmas cards. Seemed like a good idea at the time. I could talk to You about my day, all the good bits, the bad bits, and the bitchy bits. The joy in my life and the sorrow. I tried praying lying in bed, head propped up on the pillows. Sorry Lord. I've lost count how many times I've fallen asleep before saying 'Amen'. I guess a prayer interspersed with snores is a bit insulting to You. I've tried kneeling by the side of my bed. At least on my knees I cannot fall asleep. I have some wonderful purple bruises blossoming on my shins. All I can think of is how hard the floor is (despite the carpet) and how I need to brush down the cobweb that spider is weaving in the corner of the ceiling. My mind wanders, my knees hurt and I cannot pray.

So, I am writing You this letter and now it comes to it, I find there is a lot I have to say. First and foremost as a great, all-powerful, omnipotent, magnificent God, You have a lousy sense of humour. Who would have thought the twists and turns of life would have brought me here? Off I go with every intent of leading my life my way in my control and You twitch your finger and send me spinning in another direction altogether. A direction I did not choose. A life I had no desire to pursue. Of course You are right, although I have to say at the time it felt like my life was over, that everything I had fought so long and hard for, had coveted and desired, was crashing about my head. I felt exposed and vulnerable, lost and alone. I railed at You. I shook my fist at You. Now, of course, everything is grand. I have new friends, a new start, a new life. I would even tentatively suggest I am happy. I swear I hear You laughing.

Sorry God, that was a bit of a rant. I don't think you are supposed to rant at the Lord. Sometimes, God, You are a bit too cryptic for Your own good. If You do have a great master plan for me, I wish You would let me in on it from time to time. Sorry, that was another rant.

I know (despite Your chuckling) that my life has been transformed by Your interference. I know things have worked out for the best. I can see where You were coming from. You are the glory and the light. I think Your way is best. I know I should hand my life over to You. All worries, cares and troubles are safe in Your hands.

Except, except, oh God, isn't that the hardest thing to do? I decide what is best. I control the outcome. If something goes wrong it is my instinct to sort it out. I guess I am a control freak. I guess You are too, the supreme control freak. I am sorry I find it so hard to let go and pass all the worries and cares and tribulations to Your tender loving care. And, let's face it, do You really want to trouble Yourself over the dent in my car or the fence falling over? But losing my job, losing my health, is something different. I cannot sit back and wait – I have to look at alternatives, panic about the future. Oh God, I am so scared. Help me cope with this, please help me cope with this. You have guided my life in so many ways over the years, ways that felt so wrong at the time – now I see they are so right. You always seem to be there gently stroking my hair. I'll do whatever I can, but hold my hand as I do it. Guide me to the best way forward, Your way forward.

I guess at this point I ought to mention the unmitigated disaster that is my love life, or rather the absence of one. You watched how we parted and You led me here. Lord, I do love living here, even though I am on my own. I guess I am just no good with relationships, unless I just keep picking the wrong one. Oh Lord, help me find the right one. Help me be a better person. Help me learn to give and trust. Help me live my life through You.

You are glorious and wonderful and You bother with my

petty life. I am so glad that You do. I do not deserve even a glance from You. I've made so many mistakes and I am sorry for them. I will hand all of my life, not just bits of my life, to Your tender loving care. Please help me hear You and be closer to You. As I walk through this uncertain world, alone, I know I am not really alone because You are holding my hand as You walk with me. Even if You are laughing!

I don't seem to be doing this right. What was it the vicar said you had to do to pray? Praise God, thank God, confess your sins then humbly ask for something for yourself and others. Don't think I've done that very well, but then I did say right from the start I cannot pray.

Beverley Jameson

Soul Places

Soul Places
Where my soul is at home
And the longing in my soul
Is echoed and met in the lonely place –
In the wild Highlands of my Scottish forebears
Echoing down the centuries
To meet and touch the need I did not know I had.

Have You set these places, Lord?
Have You set places where our souls reach out of us
To something beyond?
Is it You calling us?
Does Your soul yearn for us
As ours yearn for You?
Have You set places where our souls can touch – Yours and
  mine?
Theologians will argue for ever over whether You even **have**
  a soul.
Does it matter what it's called
If it's that part of You which touches that part of me
In a way that is so much deeper than a kiss?

And when I was in a turmoil in the built-up South
Where the wild solitude was not open to me
You met me in watching the weir
Watching the water cauldron boil over the weir
In a never-ending torrent.
You used the watching to soothe the cauldron boil inside of me
The wild churning spoke again to me of You.

Others find these soul places in different ways.
Some find themselves meeting You
In ordered, tended gardens
Or in the paths through soft woodlands
Or in gentle rolling hills and downs
Or in the places set apart for seeking You
In buildings so soaked in prayer
That the very fabric breathes out 'Our Father' and 'Amen'.

Do You make these places, Lord
Where my soul is at home with Yours?

Beatrix Stewart

Beyond Words

Beyond words to the place where I can be without any need to find explanation for thought or action. Beyond words to the place of just being – being allowed to be just as I am, just as I feel without hesitation – spontaneous, free – free from judgement, being judged by others and judging myself. Beyond words where intellect cannot limit – where reasoning and analysing why and how I come to feel, think, behave, be, simply does not apply. Beyond words where I don't even have to think about the why and how. I don't need to have the answers. Beyond words to the place of being and of play – to play with the child and dance with Sophia – to the place of innocence and purity, a place without suspicion and guilt. Beyond words to the place of prayer and find the dwelling of the Spirit, a place where I am is just being.

E. Charlotte Wright

Encountering God in the Garden

Creating gardens has become an alluring pastime for many in the last decade. Envisioning, planning, clearing, selecting and designing are all indispensable aspects of this hobby, as well as the qualities of sheer human grit and perseverance of daily maintenance through all weathers and seasons. The gardener is rewarded with the wonder and delight of emerging beauty from the silent earth, as the myriad of plant shapes, textures and colours are gifted to the beholder. It is in that moment of awe that the heart lifts to the eternal One, for it is he who timelessly breathes inspiration and life into plant and gardener alike.

The biblical tradition tells us that nature is the handiwork of the Creator God. This foundational knowledge inspires our worship when we intentionally pause to wonder at a delicate plant, or at the majesty of a glory-filled sunset. Yet, there is a sacramental quality within the natural environment that may touch us deeply in other ways too. God mediates his very presence through nature, in such a way that we may be drawn into an experience of oneness with the created order and with God himself as Creator and Source of life.

Research into the religious experiences of two dozen people[1] confirmed many ways that their lives had been enriched spiritually, physically and emotionally through particular experiences in solitude in a natural environment. Many felt reconnected in their inner being, leading both to a deeper sense of wholeness and a renewed perspective on their lives in relation to God.

Sensual engagement with nature – looking, smelling, touching – stimulates a sense of belonging and reaching out to the Infinite. We can also discover new meanings in the transitions and seasons of our own lives if we engage with the rhythms of the natural world, whether the seasonal shifts or the lifecycle of each individual plant. Engagement with the natural order enables us to understand and interpret more richly the losses and purposes of our own fallow times, and may point us to the joys of new beginnings in the promise of spring.

If we open ourselves attentively to God in a place of natural beauty, we discover that he discloses himself to us in a sudden gift of illumination, as when we catch our breath at the unexpected fragrance of blossom. The space in which we stand becomes imbued with a deeper quality: it becomes hallowed, a place of communion, dialogue and intimacy. Whether wild or tamed, the natural world can be a context of engagement and inner transformation.

The garden itself is a microcosm of God's presence in nature. As one journalist wrote, 'the garden is not an ornament, it is a meditation'.[2] It can become a sacred place where God himself is known and made known. The garden is a metaphor frequently used in Scripture, be it the Garden of Eden or Gethsemane, and images of nature permeate descriptions of God's love relationship with his people; so we read, for example, 'You are a garden locked up, my sister my bride; you are a spring enclosed, a sealed fountain . . .' (Song of Solomon 4.12).

In the Gospels, there is a deep yet almost hidden truth – expressed in such brevity to be easily missed – that Jesus himself frequently withdrew to places of natural beauty to be still and commune with his Father. Such times undergirded his ministry, sharpening the clarity of his mission, and rooting both his activity and his very being in deep intimacy with God. Before major decisions, or after demanding periods of teaching and healing, he chose to retreat, sometimes inviting his disciples to go with him. He would seek out rest and refreshment in the open air, often in the locality. He modelled a rhythmic pattern of activity and stillness.

If he felt the need for this, should it not also be an imperative for ourselves? We are buffeted by the busyness and activism of our culture, by deadlines, by the relentless demands of a performance-based society which sap our souls of energy and distort our perspectives. By withdrawal to a place of natural beauty, we may gain a new way of seeing reality, and find restoration through the tranquillity and oneness of nature. There, in nature, God mediates new perspectives and gently re-orientates us. We become re-connected with the divine and the holy, while at the same time mysteriously drawn back into deeper involvement with the wider human community.

It therefore should not surprise us that seeds for the birth of the Quiet Garden Movement were sown in still moments of withdrawal both in places of natural beauty and those infused with the sacred. Nor need it be a surprise that those seeds, sown through three crucial experiences, took a long time to germinate.

As a fourteen-year-old, Philip Roderick, founder of the Quiet Garden Movement, lay on a cliff-top looking out over the sea, and had his first experience of 'the extraordinary otherness and yet the profound hereness of things', a felt sense of a deeper level of reality. It was only years later that he discovered that the site had been an influential monastic settlement of the Celts, a place of learning and training. Had the prayers of a monastic saint echoed through the ages to touch this young man?

A second Celtic context was also to imprint itself upon him. This time in St David's in Pembrokeshire, where as he was beginning a personal pilgrimage, he was received with warm hospitality at the hearth of an old lady. Her tiny cottage on the pilgrim's route to the cathedral was a haven of 'beauty, holiness and risk' – a meeting-place where people from many backgrounds, in sharing their stories, found peace and sanctuary. The vision of a network of pilgrim centres providing a context for prayer and hospitality was slowly being birthed in Philip's heart.

In 1992 a rich sabbatical of learning and experience enabled him to clarify and articulate this vision. Its essence was to endorse and honour deeply the contemplative dimension within our active lives by the provision of local homes and gardens as places of refreshment, prayer and hospitality. The dream was to become a reality when a group of committed and busy Christians, who also seriously desired to find the balance between the active and the contemplative felt called to pursue this vision with commitment and effort. A couple in Stoke Poges in Buckinghamshire generously agreed to make available their delightful home and garden to be the pilot project for this new venture. Thus the first Quiet Garden was born!

Initially, the Quiet Garden offered two days a week for

periods of teaching, quiet prayer, meditation and sharing. Teaching drew from the riches of the Judaeo-Christian tradition, to be found in such saints and mystics as Teresa of Avila, Thomas Merton, and the Celtic Christians, or it was combined with other media such as poetry or music. There was always plenty of silence for meditative reflection and prayer.

Such was the interested response that it became clear there was a demand for this kind of ministry, and others began to offer their homes to be used in similar ways. The basic model was easily replicable around the world and totally flexible to meet the particular needs of the locality. It is also a low-cost way of providing a local sacred space for spiritual nurture, prayer and companionship.

Every Quiet Garden is unique in what it offers with regard to availability, content and space. One might simply provide a context for listening prayer, another offer a mini-retreat or teaching. Always, the need of the individual is respected, be it for silence and stillness, or a listening, companionable ear.

In 1994, after the firm grounding of the pilot project at Stoke Poges, the Quiet Garden Trust was established to co-ordinate the growth of the ministry. The Trust is able to advise those considering opening a Quiet Garden and offers pastoral support. In God's timing, those initial precious seeds burst forth and Quiet Gardens sprang up in many different contexts, as others caught the vision and offered their own homes and gardens for the common purpose of creating a context for spiritual transformation and refreshment. Growth was dramatic: by 1995 there were forty Quiet Gardens rising to two hundred and fifty-five worldwide in early 2003. It has become an international and ecumenical venture as the seeds were carried to far-flung places in Asia, North and South America, Africa, Australia and New Zealand.

The organic growth of the movement has therefore been startling. From the initial vision based on private homes and gardens in rural and urban locations alike, the idea expanded to the provision of quiet spaces in more public arenas and workplaces. As this idea fired the imagination of others, Quiet Gardens and Quiet Spaces began to be established in churches, schools, hospitals and retreat houses.

Today, the Quiet Gardens show enormous diversity, and in the UK range from a small terraced house in Windsor under the Heathrow flight path, a rediscovered Victorian garden providing a picturesque and secluded oasis of natural beauty at Worth Abbey, a tiny hermitage in Bristol, and a drug rehabilitation centre in London, to the cottage gardens of a reconciliation project in Northern Ireland.

Further afield in Kampala, Uganda, on the edge of a busy hospital, there is a Quiet Garden filled with aromatic and healing herbs. Here at the Nsambya Clinic, weary AIDS workers, close to burn-out with an overwhelming number of patients with HIV/AIDS, find a calm place for recovery and meditation. In India, an organisation caring for commercial sex workers and their families runs two Quiet Gardens in the red-light district of a sprawling city of Maharashtra State. In contrast, the Olive Branch Retreat is a Quiet Garden overlooking the tranquil bay at Mangonui, a small fishing village in the far north of New Zealand. The garden gives opportunity for reflection and contemplation, while a self-contained studio gives the possibility of a longer stay.

The essential vision behind the Quiet Garden movement balances the needs of the inner journey with vigorous outward movement to share the whole concept – a pattern that mirrors the gospel imperative.

Nowhere demonstrates this more clearly than the project for a Quiet Garden in the village of Torbeck, Haiti. A small group of adults and teenagers from two Quiet Gardens in Kansas made a trip to Haiti to help create a garden which would become an oasis of rest and refreshment for a bustling church compound. The church is the scene of constant activity, be it teaching, medical work or mission visits. The project itself was a delightful example of partnership and cooperation as black and white hands removed wheelbarrows of rocks and pebbles, planted beautiful begonias, and constructed a simple wooden bench to provide a resting-place in the shade. Teenagers from Kansas working with the Haitian youth had children and gardenworkers make their handprints on the bench to make a truly 'hand-some' bench! This Quiet Garden, established in love, is now a sanctuary enabling local and foreigner alike to pause, to wonder at the beauty of God's creation and just to 'be'. Haiti, while being poor materially, thus extends a rich gift of hospitality!

The creation of another Quiet Garden, in London, symbolises the fresh possibilities of change within our own inner journeys. Interested local inhabitants and parishioners at St Matthew's Church, Camberwell, saw the dramatic transformation of a rough, derelict and barren site into a glorious quiet space. God provided not only willing helpers but also offers of help from unexpected quarters to remove rubble from an old shed and to donate plants. A brick wall received inspirational painting in both subtle and vibrant colours, the garden became a series of 'rooms' to suit different moods, and brick beds were prepared for climbing plants. In 1997, the garden was officially opened and how appropriate that the address was titled 'Praying from the mess of things'! Places of stillness and beauty do not shield us from the daily struggles of life, but they provide a symbol of God's presence in the ordinary.

Nor is it only the visitor who is blessed in the garden. As Philip Roderick wrote, 'One home-owner in Canada had worked hard on his garden for ten years. He and his wife opened up their home on a monthly basis as a Quiet Garden. On the first day of their programme, he found himself with tears in his eyes, sitting on one of the benches he had fashioned, looking at one of the trees he had planted the year before. He realised suddenly that this was the first time that he had stopped working **on** his garden and given himself permission simply to contemplate and delight **in** it.'[3]

Children too have a deep capacity to appreciate stillness. The pupils at St Michael's School in Devon delight in their Quiet Space, the Orchard, which has been created for their well-being. They have shared the following comments about what this stillness means to them: 'Quiet areas offer us peace and quiet, time to relax away from being busy, give space so we can think and concentrate our own thoughts, help us to see more and to listen, move and discover more.'

The potency of the Quiet Garden is therefore not in its size, or its tidiness or even its crafting, but in the silent witness of creation, mediating stillness and the presence of God. The

POINTS OF LIGHT

Quiet Garden provides a calm place where chores and agendas can be set on one side so that the 'still, small voice' of God may be heard and balance restored to body, mind and soul. May the Quiet Gardens remain sacred places where, by drawing closer to the living God, child, pilgrim, stranger and friend find restoration and renewal of hope.

Mollie Robinson

1 Janet Ruffing, **The Presence** 3.1 (1997).
2 **Gardening Which**, June 2001, p. 253.
3 **The Way Supplement** '99/95 p. 71.

DISCOVERING
FAITH Stations
THROUGH

Stations

The concept of Stations of the Cross evolved during the late
Middle Ages as a form of devotion. Each stage of Christ's walk
to his crucifixion becomes a focus for deep meditation. It
provides an opportunity for us all to walk the Via Dolorosa in
Jerusalem, to in some way engage in this journey that is
central to the belief of Christians.

This sequence of incidents, the people who took part and
those who observed, the small details that enhance the overall
event, all have had immense appeal for visual artists, com-
posers, dramatists, film-writers, prose-writers and poets. Sometimes it is as if all this going towards death is the slow-motion
summary of the meaning and culmination of the life of Christ.

The story, its significance and the concept continues to
challenge. Tony Lucas has written a sequence of fourteen,
fourteen-line verses, the focus being on the traditional incidents. The story is told in today's language.

E. Charlotte Wright's twelve paintings have evolved from
recent photo-journalism. Our own world connects with this
old narrative and moves on, transforming and yet still challenged. The final sequence of poems in response to these
paintings takes 'Stations' as points of recognition, places where
we start and stop, meet and greet, wait and then journey on.

Disclosure: Like Us

Inspired by the Stations of the Cross, this group of twelve paintings looks at the depths and heights of our human nature and vulnerability. Most of them have evolved from the photo-journalism of recent events, particularly in the Holy Land. The paintings relate to the emotional life of Christ and the people around him, especially in the final days of his life recorded in the Gospels.

The paintings are iconistic in that they have the potential to be windows of meaning. In them, our own experiences and vulnerabilities can find identity and value in the humanity of Christ. The people whose expressions and gestures fill the paintings weave their own stories with the story of Christ's Passion. All of them come together to disclose a transformative journey from suffering into growth and new beginnings.

The choice of colours in the originals was largely influenced by religious Orthodox icon-painting with other ideas coming from Kitaj, with regard to his approach to his own work, Rodin's sculptural poses and Oulton's textural surfaces. The uncomplicated structures of the paintings contrast with the complexity of ideas and emotions they represent.

E. Charlotte Wright

1 **Malkutha** – from the Aramaic, whose meaning refers to a guiding royalty which permeates the universe. It is what says 'I can' within us and is willing, despite all odds, to take a step in a new direction. When Christ battled with his emotions in Gethsemane, perhaps this quality strengthened him to do what he must.

2 **Embrace** – Bush and Putin embracing at a political summit is merely coincidental, but their pose interprets as the embrace of a friend betrayed, whoever it may be, and is the link for Christ embracing Judas. The mauve-pink colour in the original is the colour of the Judas tree's blossom, in flower during my visit to the Holy Land in March 2002.

3 **Denial** – a paedophile hides his face with his hand from the world press. His pose becomes the model for Peter, who denied Christ three times. It serves to remind us of all forms of denial in relationships.

4 **Accused** – David Beckham, who stood silently with his team in memory of Holly Wells and Jessica Chapman, inspired the pose for Christ accused by his people. His bowed posture can speak for the pain of all those unjustly accused or restrained.

5 **Bonnie's Cry** – Palestinian women and children fleeing the guns in Gaza and a European girl grieving over her football team losing in the World Cup have been the inspiration for the composition of this painting. It relates to Christ speaking to the women of Jerusalem, when he told them not to cry for him, but for themselves and their children. Bonnie was an American Christian nurse who worked in the Lebanon with Palestinian refugee women and children. She was gunned down by a terrorist.

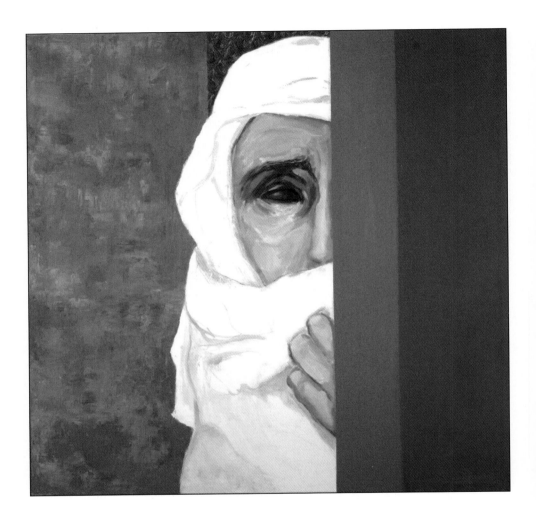

6 **Mother** – An elderly Palestinian woman in the West Bank, her eyes full of all that she has seen and is seeing, becomes the model for the mother of Christ as she stands from a distance watching her son die. For all mothers who watch their children suffer.

7 **Helper** – A Jewish father mourns at the graveside of his daughter, killed in a suicide bombing, and is helped by someone close by who comforts him. Simon of Cyrene, pulled in from the crowd as a convenient source of strength, became a helper when he was made to carry the cross for the weakening Christ.

8 **Return** – The pose relates to a granddaughter rushing to greet her grandfather as he is released from prison and speaks of reunion and return. Christ spoke to the thief crucified with him, promising that 'today' he would be with him in paradise. He would be returning to be reunited as a child to its father. The theme extends in this painting to one of global reunion and reconciliation.

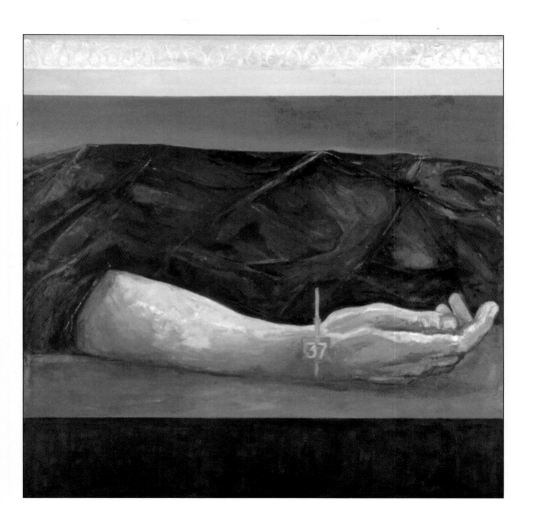

9 **Victim 37** – The Stations of the Cross, which confront the death and burial of Christ, are universal in that each of us will be touched by grief and death at some time or other. The victim in this painting is the result of another suicide bombing in Jerusalem.

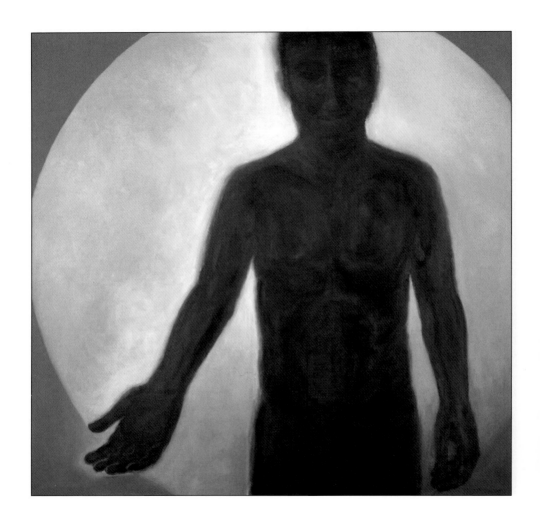

10 **Dayspring** – A figure comes towards us, silhouetted dark against the bright dawn light. His open hand is outstretched, almost beckoning. The need for new dawns, new beginnings, free and unfettered by the past, can find fresh meaning in the Resurrection of Christ. 'The old has passed away, behold the new has come' (2 Corinthians 5.17; Paul quoting Isaiah).

11 **Way Forward** – A footballer strongly and convincingly points the way ahead to victory after his winning goal. His gesture speaks of confidence, faith and joy. Such people exude energy and encouragement. The disciples of Christ knew him as 'the Way'. We too may reflect on the way forward as we consider these qualities.

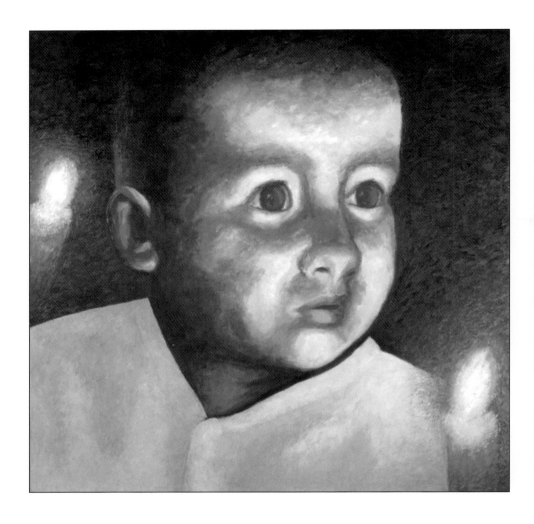

12 **Epiphany** – A small child in Delhi watches at a candlelight vigil for peace between India and Pakistan, his young eyes focused and aware, perhaps seeing with the beginnings of understanding. Epiphany comes from the Greek 'phaino', 'to show'. The Magi were shown and understood the Christ child, heralded as the Prince of Peace.

Stations

*A poem sequence in response to the paintings by
E. Charlotte Wright*

I

You have to decide, don't you?
Between the lies that are told
and the way that words can turn
the world upside down and
the taunting silences.

You have to determine once and for all, don't you?
What we have been told and what we have received
and what jumps from our own mouths.
Words as nails. Words as weapons. Words as wounds.
Words that get stuck in the head and nothing, nothing,
    nothing

will drive them out. At Gethsemane. At this point
of no return. At this time which can never be repeated
with a prayer bleeding in the brain. All that has gone before
is blood knowledge, blood narrative, blood idea;
over now.

II

Colour of the Judas tree, traitor's blossom,
ruin robe, terror coat.

What it is to change sides; one minute my brother,
the next delivering me.

I kiss you now because I have to.
I kiss you now because you have all the time known.

I kiss you to kill you.

Now.

III

Denial is so very easy. We do this in the head
all the time. We put on a suit to lie. We turn
things round and inside out and hide and seeking
we become so many other things. And it is
done so easily.

And then we move on to the next bit, to deny
the denial. We put on a hat to hide the lie;
changing games, changing names, changing
what we have already changed.

Look; I can do it with my eyes closed, I don't
even have to think about it. Over and over
until even I don't know quite what
might happen next.

We put up a hand to hide the face to
hide the eyes to deny the lie
that never took place.

IV

All the voices begin to sound the same voice
and the words are at war;
sling shots, knuckles, fists, wires spinning
in the mind, looting logic, cascading blame

and nobody listens.

Whatever you might say
there is no point in replying;
replying is lying.

Whatever words might be used
silence is better
until silence is denial.

And prayer; what could a prayer do, be, become
when you already know how this story will end?

Their hands have become claws.

V

I want to tell you but my mouth will not.
Everything has already changed
and whatever I might say
is silenced by terror, by the actual,
by the stone moment.

The mothers are stone. The children are stone.
The baby is now a stone baby.

The stone baby will become a stone child
will become a stone adult
and pray to a stone god.

I want to tell you but my
scream
has become
stone.

VI

When you are no longer running at the sun,
when you are no longer chasing birds,
when you are no longer testing us and teasing,
when you are no longer trying out the words,
when you are no longer amazing us,
when you are no longer radiant

I your mother have to watch you stumble,
have to observe you torn,
have to see you broken.

The soldiers who do this have mothers.
The soldiers who do this have children.

What will they tell them about today?

VII

And yet they come to comfort,
they come with a story,
they enter the darkest room seeking
the point of light that is always there
real or imagined or.

And the words are bread
and the words are water
and

VIII

. . . millions are moving. If you are an angel
you can hear them and know their stories and dreams.
At night their souls always return to the place
their bodies left. At night they always manage
to get back to mothers and brothers and the children
run between the rivers that are beautiful.
Sometimes they can achieve this during the day,
even as they hide and scream and fall in pain,
even as the soldiers spit at them and kill them.
And when they are dead they have already reached
the other place, the other language, the bodies
set aside and the soul leaping to another song.
. . . millions are moving. If you are an angel
you know their names.

IX

In a body bag there is all the time
in and out. The ultimate void.
The inside story.
And nobody is listening.

What comes next is a miracle of course.
What doesn't happen is also a miracle
and the bits in between.

The body and its wounds and its gradual
escape from form. The mind also escaping
and the soul already released.

The silence. Light lifting everything
already beyond anything we have
ever known.

All the words. All the texts.
All the earth knowledge now transcending
beyond light and its measurements,
beyond meaning.

God's hands already holding.

X

This is a man who is dressed in the eyes of God;
This is a man who is rising in realms of light;
This is a man who has attended the birthday of pain.

What will you say to us
and how shall we perceive your wonders?

I am a carol hidden between planets;
I am a song that is ancient yet unborn;
I am exile and angel.

I forgive you all.

XI

Outside the ruined tea room in Kabul
the balloon man has returned.
After the bombing, after the punishment,
the balloon man comes to sell again
these radiances that do not explode,
do not carry fire, do not enter caves,
do not search,
do carry messages.

XII

In the meningitis ward the Irish nuns never leave them.
Sometimes they work for sixteen hours at a stretch.
When this young boy arrived with his dying mother in a
    basket
nobody had time to hear his story. There was no room.
Every story that has ever been told already whispers here.
So he told nobody about the first deaths; his father and
    uncle,
and then living in the forest and the sounds of soldiers and
    animals.
So he told nobody about his brothers and what happened to
    their hands
and the rape of his sister and the four months of running
    between
one slaughter and another. So he told nobody about how
    they
gave up words, signalled in silence, eating rain.
Now, in this meningitis ward, he makes up a story as his
mother dies, he places a prayer in the singing, he holds
her hands in the music and she is dead now.
He covers the body on the mat with leaves to hide the smell
that has been in his head for months.
He tells an Irish nun that he will stay here
with these people he does not know.
'I can work. I can do singing. I can do peace.'

David H. W. Grubb

1 Before Pilate

The more uncertain an intended verdict
then the more precise court rituals need
to be. It never helps to get a prisoner
who goes mute, who challenges the court.

What is truth? The truth is this performance
all needs paying for. It's taking up
important people's time. Justice is only
cost-effective where it helps forestall
expensive breakdowns of the peace.

Take nothing at face value. Terms such as
'guilt' and 'innocence' are technical.
The accused is a symbolic figure. Shrewd minds
know roles can be reversed, so what gets put
on trial is the whole elaborate show.

2 He Accepts his Cross

Sign along the bottom – here and here.
This is government property you're being issued.
All has to be accounted for. Good timber
has its price. I wouldn't trust the local
carpenters. Also this one, if you will – confirms
that you were read your rights. Just covers us
if anyone should bring complaints.

No point being difficult today. The choice
you have is go with dignity, or else
be dragged. We do have ways to make it
that bit easier for prisoners who co-operate.
Look at it this way – nobody chooses to be
born. At least you've got the chance to make
a good impression by the way you die.

DISCOVERING FAITH THROUGH

3 The First Fall

Even the emblematic cross that's carried
ecumenically around suburban streets
on damp Good Fridays – couple of lengths
of two-by-four cobbled together – even that
will bear acutely on an unaccustomed
collar-bone, will cut more sharply in
the shoulder of a volunteer with every
step he takes – though coming nowhere near
the substance to support a human frame.

The bruised, whipped body of a beaten man
– no matter that he used to tramp the hills,
or grew up hefting timber – would quickly
find the imposition of this final
straw more than enough to break him down.

4 Simon of Cyrene

Never the safest place for tourists. A noisy
crowd coming through old Jerusalem –
better move quickly than stand by to watch
the show. A sergeant with three prisoners to get
through narrow streets, an edgy crowd, when one
of the condemned collapses. What does he do?

Glance round the hostile faces, spot the big African
who looks a bit bemused, conscript him to
the action. Don't argue with a Roman sword.
The man complies – hoping they'll keep track
of who is who. The way it all turned out
was strange – not making him like the Romans, yet
something about that prisoner made it feel
almost right that he should be on hand.

5 Veronica

Patron saint of **paparazzi** –
she was right there, following
the action, getting up close – all about
good timing. She got the picture.

This is the image that will fill
front pages, wired by the agencies
world wide, be on the tee-shirts,
launching a thousand icons.

All he has left to give now is
the grime that blinds him. Imprint
of sweat and blood and dust wiped
on a headscarf: chemicals on paper,
contact with history, trick of the light –
it is the image that can steal the soul.

6 The Second Fall

Well, what did he expect? Coming here
telling us how to live our lives,
trying to say what's right and wrong,
as if we'd not been properly brought up.
Healing the cripples, lunatics,
making it look as if we didn't take
good care of them ourselves. Breaking
the rules, twitting the lawyers, eating
and drinking with fat quislings, while
he told us we should give away
our second coat, or not get even for
some sleight. Made you feel mean, having
a bit more than the lot next door. No,
don't look for sympathy. It serves him right.

7 Women of Jerusalem

Don't you just hate audience participation?
Actors turning on the people in the front row
asking us what we mean by being there,
saying that this was never meant to be
a picture that we're looking at – more like
a mirror held up to the muddle of
our own confusions and duplicity?

Without spectators there can't be a show.
Why make the worshippers uncomfortable?
Fingers point through the screen. This green-stick
fracture of the frame that comes between
us and the emblematic drama causes
the wood, that superstitiously we touch,
to splinter and get underneath the skin.

8 The Third Fall

They say that Adam's apple was a pip
stuck in his throat, grown to a tree above
his grave. Cut as the plank that Sheba couldn't
walk, raised in the Temple, later buried
in a healing spring. He bears it now,
the second Adam. If the first one fell
on his feet, knowing both good and evil, work
and love, the burden weighs this new man down.

In others' eyes, the beam looks foolish. He has
no fear of letting weakness show, no need
for saving face, while facing up to tough
demands, like matching freedom with integrity.
Here is permission to break down,
sign of the fall, the rising up of many.

9 Stripped of his Garments

He had no interest in possession, merely
footwear, one good shift someone had made
for him, but took his chances with the rest.
He could sleep anywhere, soft beds or ditches,
relished good food when it was offered, but
could walk all through the day, not break
his fast. He'd done time in the wilderness.

People liked giving to him – always seemed
to get more in return. Most, though, took from him,
– his word, his time, his privacy, his touch.
As if he always was aware the day
for disinvestment had to come, it seemed
he carefully secured his poverty,
assured of having nothing left to lose.

10 Nailed to the Cross

Nailing sound wood should be a satisfying
task, clinching a well-judged fit in true
alignment. To nail down flesh is botchers'
work, messy and imprecise, wrong methods
for the wrong materials. It can't offer
the reward of finding neat solutions,
the assurance of a job well done.

It all comes down to oozing, shouting, down to
cursing and the mess. You can bodge up
something that will last a few hours, will
achieve its short-term purpose; but there's no
aesthetic. This is an ugly business, lacking
all pretence to proper workmanship,
nothing that will stand the test of time.

11 The Mother

The company of weeping mothers – vast
unlooked-for fellowship that threads through history,
searching the battlefields, queuing at prison gates,
lining the route to executions. Sometimes
they put a stop to wars, sometimes begin them.
They bring down governments, they fuel vendetta.

We picture her the quiet victim, patiently
suffering her pain for greater purposes –
yet place a Magdalene beside herself,
distraught, nails clawing at the air in outrage.

The mother stands. This time, at least, she knew.
At least there was a body to be buried,
close companions who would not forget,
witnesses who'd see it didn't end at this.

12 Dies on the Cross

That's really done it now. However much
you thought that's what you wanted, you will find
it wasn't what you meant at all. Death changes
everything. Common assault shifts to
a capital offence. Some trouble-maker,
minor irritant, becomes transformed
into a potent martyr, emblem round which
thousands will cohere, rise up against you.

Blood runs and sticks on many fingers. Guilt
respects no boundary of law or status.
Blood cries aloud, will not be covered up,
or brazened out, or washed away. The inquiry
could go on for years, for centuries.
Only return to innocence is barred.

13 Taken Down from the Cross

You've seen the pictures – two people stuck
up a ladder, juggling the stiff and awkward body
in mid-air. You'd have to say that there are
health and safety issues here. Soldiers, perhaps,
can execute the task with a professional
aplomb. But, left to amateurs, the piety,
emotional involvement, will betray them
into clumsiness and silly risks.

Under the press of such affliction, even
the circumspect break cover, out of a need
to see the right thing done, even if
it means wrong people doing it. Taking
any action in the face of the unthinkable
steps beyond helplessness, moves things on.

14 Laid in the Tomb

They do the decent thing – show what respect
seems practical in awkward circumstances,
even at certain risk to reputations.

Sometimes the dead won't act responsibly,
lie there in proper peace under their stones.
We fix them down with monuments, plant
flowers and tributes, but our guilts, our hopes
and fears leave open fissures that we fail
to seal. So they come back to interrupt
our lives, direct, impose their stern demands.

Now, in the early half-light, spices meant
to sweeten the decay are scattered, guards
desert their post, three frightened women leave
their footprints running in the morning dew.

Tony Lucas

DISCOVERING
FAITH
THROUGH Music &
Dance &

Music and Dance

The role of music and dance as integral elements in Christian religious expression was once far more significant than it is today. It was essence, an outgoing expression of energy within, something that went beyond words and even precise interpretation.

It is evident from wall paintings, sculpture and spoken narratives that in pre-Christian times music and dance went deeper than ritual.

Music and in particular song still hold a prominent position and strong popular appeal. The psalms, choirs, incantation and music-making remain part of religious expression and many would argue that for young people music offers the most attractive celebrations and the most accessible routes to spiritual participation, challenge and awareness.

Dance as a revelation of the spiritual self, as an expression of journeying, delight and desire for truth, has largely lost its place in Western worship. We dance in our hearts and heads but leave no room for dancing bodies. The orthodoxy of worship forms and the architecture of religious buildings is fundamental to the problem. The exceptions are bold and brilliant and mostly relate to young people who reject such constraints and create their own spaces and forms.

One of the major challenges facing the formal church structure is how to let today's light in, today's souls in, today's radiances and energies in.

Tune me, O Lord, into one harmony
With Thee, one full responsive vibrant chord;
Unto Thy praise, all love and melody,
Tune me, O Lord.

Christina Rossetti

Only let me make my life simple and straight like a flute of reed for Thee to fill with music.

Anonymous

Some Reflections about Music as Prayer

Music is a unique activity we are born to refine and express. We learn rhythm from the night and the day, we learn pitch from the voices of our father and mother heard from within the womb. We learn pulse from life itself pulsing within us. From baby songs and rhymes we learn love, and the music we learn to sing and play (for those of us lucky enough to have an instrument, however simple) both expresses us and changes us. We open our very beings – physically, emotionally and intellectually – to music, and it re-orders us. It is a kind of prayer. A saint once said that those who sing pray twice over: the prayer becomes our breath and heartbeat. The milkman's heartbeat changes as he whistles a lovesong, and those who pray in song become their prayer in flesh and spirit. Even those reciting the psalms in rhythm become held, poised in space, as the silence between the phrases hangs in the air. (For silence is held by music.)

I have recently learned to sing, and more recently learned to play the violin. Both demanded a new musical skill that I had not learned as a pianist: to listen and adjust – constantly, accurately and critically – the tuning of both voice and strings. No piano tuner to come round every six months to do the work for me. Tuning becomes the main task. And it is a profoundly spiritual one because it means listening for a sound you have yet to make, and trying to play it truly. You must constantly listen, and reject false notes. In singing, only extra energy will stop you going, just detectably, flat.

George Herbert, himself a string player, wrote of being out of tune, and being retuned by God, and it's hardly surprising that 'harmony' is one of our favourite metaphors for our relationships with God and each other. We recognize diversity, but we long for the harmony that celebrates the diversity and yet resolves it into some beautiful cadence, perhaps more beautiful and satisfying because of the disharmony that comes before.

If we are searching for a way of existing that communicates and integrates, we have a perfect model in making music: it both stretches and integrates our selves – in body, mind and spirit – and also joins us to others, and moves us to seek and express the absolute relationships of sound that Leonard Bernstein proposes in his Harvard lectures on music, 'The Unanswered Question?' The mathematical logic and structure of sound and its beauty, makes him believe in the metaphysical reality of absolute beauty and truth, accessible to us through musical form.

Reflections on Dance as Prayer

Dance was once every child's birthright, and it was theirs until they became too old or too ill to do more than feel their pulse quicken or their eyes dance to the rhythm of pattern and line. Rhythm, pattern and line are the stuff of Creation – and built into our bodies. It became part of our social fabric to express every emotion, every stage in life, the seasons and times. It was fun.

Now dance is just a metaphor in the West – a very fashionable metaphor for spiritual freedom, one you'll find in every publisher's list of new titles. But most people leave dance to the professionals. It is embarrassing, exposing, shameful, difficult. It needs special, expensive spaces, and special shoes. It has connotations of sexual display. Still, there are people who dance, and who dance when they pray.

I dance on Mondays with a ring of people, mostly older, a few younger, and we dance dances from around the world. We learn the dances of ancient communities, some of which were danced by Jesus himself at weddings and celebrations, or dances that holiday-makers may find themselves dancing in tavernas on a Greek island, or in Romania, Bulgaria or Macedonia. We arrive tired, and sometimes feeling under the weather, but in the circle we create an energy together that is focused on a candle, the light of the world. At the end, we send that light to those who need it, and we ourselves are refreshed, healed and lightened. Sometimes we dance the dances of Kosovo, Serbia and Russia and pray as our feet tread out their patter. Sometimes we dance leaping, singing dances of South Africa, and learn to praise God in that way. The steps are simple enough for women in their eighties, and light enough for a girl in her teens. In themselves they are nothing, but together, we weave satisfying patterns, and we give ourselves entirely to the dance, the light and the circle for as long as it lasts.

On Tuesday I put on tap shoes and dance with all the laid-back joy of the USA. The rhythmic complexity cuts across and complements the music with another layer, bringing out rhythms in it that were there but unheard until my feet describe them. Together or alone, we think of nothing else but the syncopated patter which is so rich and fun. I praise God in the rhythm of my feet.

On Wednesday I remember and restate the lessons of ballet, which train the body and soul up towards a nobility and grace that isn't seen in ordinary life except in the goodness of saints, who never lose their centre, who never put a foot wrong, wobble, trip or fall. Marvin Hamlisch's characters sing 'Everything is beautiful at the ballet' because they were captivated by the romance of the studios, the security of technique and the perfection that the plainest, most unloved child could strive for. But I can no longer achieve the total release of technique perfectly mastered, and this is a spiritual memory for me, remembered by muscles, but no longer executed by them.

On Thursday I make different moves. Tai Chi is both discipline and freedom, describing arcs and lines in silent space. Are these movements for pleasure and beauty or defence and violent speed-in-slow-motion? Body and spirit come together again, as I consciously change weight, step out, step back, seeking balance, to open the body, to wait. These are lessons for life.

Terence Handley MacMath

DISCOVERING
FAITH
THROUGH Questions &
Responses &

Questions and Responses

Those contributing to this anthology were asked to consider their personal responses to Ten Questions about Prayer and Praying.

What follows demonstrates positive diversity to something that we may participate in regularly, formally and informally, or something that is occasional and cautious, and seldom final.

Some of the contributors did not respond in print. Praying itself takes us to the edge of our human rationality and that is enough. For many readers this may also be true. One can provide the details of each element in a stained-glass window or the partitions of a tapestry, but never the light-enhancing, revealing wholeness.

Following these responses, in the final section of this book there are suggested topics for individual reflection and group discussion: on prayers in the Bible, the power and place of the Psalms, the way in which Jesus used prayer, and the original perceptions of praying.

If a prayer can be seen as a signature of our faith, what does a prayer say of us?

Ten Questions about Prayers and Praying

1 Is the concept of prayer and praying rational?
2 When you pray, in private or with others, what do you believe you are doing?
3 What do you think of 'results' or 'responses' to praying?
4 How hard is it to pray?
5 Do you pray with forms other than silence or words?
6 Can you name a prayer composed by someone else by title and author's name?
7 Is there a piece of music or a building, a poem or a work of art that comes near to being a prayer in itself?
8 Has there ever been a time in your life when you deliberately gave up praying?
9 Can wit or irony or humour be part of a prayer?
10 Is there anything else you would like to say about prayer or praying?

Responses

1 Given that I have never doubted the existence of God it seems to me to be entirely rational that I should speak to Him – after all, I speak to everyone else.
2 Communicating with God/Jesus.
3 I'm not sure I understand this question. Certainly in my experience prayer is answered (sometimes with an answer I don't want) – is this what is meant by 'results'? If so, then results happen, but not always in a way that was expected.
4 Very hard and as easy as breathing. Often it is an automatic response, but making time to sit down and spend time with God/Jesus is not so easy. Talking to Him is easy, especially when I have a lot to say, but making myself stop to listen for the answer can be very hard indeed, especially if I think I will receive an answer I don't want.
5 Yes. I sometimes pray with dance and often when singing.
6 Yes – The Lord's Prayer by Jesus, 'Make me a channel' by St Francis of Assisi, 'Oh Holy Jesus' by Richard of Chichester.

These are three that come to mind straight away. If I thought about it I could probably think of more.

7 Yes. Many hymns are prayers; and pieces of music, for example, by J. S. Bach, and poems definitely. I am less moved by architecture so to me buildings as prayers do not spring to mind.

8 No.

9 Definitely. God most certainly has a sense of humour and it's fun sharing mine with Him.

10 If you haven't tried it, why not give it a go? You may feel foolish if you are not sure anyone is there, but what have you got to lose?

〰〰〰

1 The concept of prayer is highly irrational – if rationality is defined by that which can be perceived by the senses and/or measured – but that does not mean it doesn't obey scientific laws, particularly the laws of causality.

2 Prayer is a method of connecting with the unseen universe.

3 On this one, I believe the old adage, 'Ask and you shall receive'. I believe that the universe provides for us: that we get everything that we ask for, always. The only trouble is our minds are constantly asking for all sorts of stuff that we don't need; and also, our minds are full of contradictions (thus we cancel out the power of this asking). Prayer, like meditation, is a way of becoming single-minded, focusing the power of this asking.

4 Becoming single-minded is very difficult indeed. However, if you are the sort of person that needs a personal Jesus or saviour, belief in this saviour and his or her ability to remonstrate with God on your behalf can be a very powerful tool. Christians (even those of the narrow-minded, bigoted, holier-than-thou school) are generally better at 'miracles' than open-minded, non-aligned, spiritually inclined people.

5 I believe that one can get to the stage where every breath,

every step, every smile, every meal, every song is a prayer. Sadly, I'm far from being there yet, but I try.

6 I believe 'The Prophet' by Kahlil Gibran to be a prayer (as I understand prayer to be).

7 Many. The paintings of Marc Chagall come to mind immediately, even the abstract window/door paintings of Rothko are a prayer. Musically, we might be inclined to think of Mozart's or Verdi's requiems as prayers, but in truth, I think Fatboy Slim got closer to the mark with 'Praise You' (which I'm sure was written for Zoë Ball rather than Jesus). Any music that sends you into a trance or makes you feel connected with others (no matter how fleeting the feeling) is a prayer. Techno is a prayer.

8 I gave up praying at the age of eight when I tested God out by swearing at him and he didn't strike me down. I gave up 'Christianity' shortly afterwards. Twenty-two years later I had a road-to-Damascus type of experience in which – among other things – I discovered my abilities as a spiritual healer. Since then I have worked with meditation and prayer (but not under the auspices of an organised or even a disorganised religion).

9 Wit or irony are part of our everyday lives (unless you are pious and holier-than-thou) and therefore can be part of our prayers too. I also believe they are an essential tool for questionnaires.

10 Do not pray for ease, comfort or happiness, but for freedom, understanding and compassion: for disease/unease, discomfort and unhappiness are often great motivators.

〰〰〰

I can't answer all the questions, but I have to address the eighth first. I was brought up a Methodist, going to Sunday School every week, and saying my prayers before I was tucked up in bed at night. I also sang hymns and said prayers at school every schoolday.

8 I don't remember. I remember that my parents lost their faith in their local church because of some things that

happened. But does a teenager need an excuse to stop praying at bedtime?

4 It is very hard to pray, especially when there is no body or thing or entity or 'god' to which one can pray. I thought (and think). But it's not that I don't want to pray. And there have been numerous times when praying seemed like all there was.

2 There has been one occasion in the last few years when I have prayed. I don't know who or what I was praying to, but I know I needed to pray. Was it rational (Question 1)? I don't know. Probably not. But it was all I had.

〰〰〰

1 a) If by rational we mean 'reasoned out', it is likely that many highly intuitive people do not pray rationally: they just do it, in unconsidered response to a deep and urgent feeling that it is the right, necessary and appropriate thing to do in their particular situation.

There are other people whose personality distrusts intuition, and prefers action in response to logical analysis of the available options. Such people will probably pray in response to a deep, carefully thought-out conviction that prayer is what is required of them at that time. Their prayer is rational, in this sense.

Both are God's children. There is no reason to think that one sort of prayer is inherently better, worse, more effective, more readily heard by God, than the other. He made us different from each other, to do different sorts of work for Him during our earthly lives. And He loves and listens to all of us, when we pray in the name of Our Lord Jesus and in acknowledgement of God's existence and greatness.

b) If the question were to be interpreted to mean, 'Is it rational to pray?', other factors become relevant.

Prayer results from faith that God does exist. If He exists, and is the loving Father whom Our Lord Jesus showed to us in His earthly life, then it is clearly rational for us to pray to him. This is our means of communicating our concerns and confusions to Him, receiving His directions to us, and the assurance of His loving care for us (see 2 over page).

Since we humans cannot see or touch God, we cannot prove His existence, or otherwise, by scientific means. We can only believe or disbelieve that He does exist.

Such belief is called 'faith', and is a gift from God, constantly on offer to everyone whom He has created. The nature of the development of each individual's faith is a result of how readily, and in what way, individuals allow themselves to perceive and accept that gift, the individual's readiness to 'let God into one's soul'.

Some people find themselves 'letting God in' all of a sudden. Many others are more determined to resist God, and the growth of their faith is gradual, over months, or even years.

Among other things (notably, influences from other people, and the occurrence of particular experiences), the 'readiness to let God in' is also a function of each individual's personality. People whose personality is predominantly intuitive 'know' God exists. People whose personality is predominantly 'judgemental' may resist that acceptance of God until they can find a 'rational' (i.e. reasoned out) structure in which to recognise Him and His relationship with themselves.

The basis of such a rational structure seems to me to lie in the facts that:

- no one can say who caused the 'Big Bang' beginning of Creation: in the absence of any other explanation, it seems likely that there is an unimaginably powerful being out there who was responsible – let us call Him God.
- everything seems to have its own particular part to play in the logical organisation which we call Creation (our studies of this are called 'ecology'), and to have its own logical purpose: surely, humanity's purpose must be more than to live a muddled, confused, earthly life of physical danger, mental distress and occasional short-

lived happiness – there must be a life after death, presumably closer to our creator God.

- Jesus was a historical character, as real and as well recorded as King Alfred or Edward the Confessor; much of what Jesus told us about God fits in with our previous logical conclusions – why should we doubt the extra bits He told us about God's love for His Created creatures, and God's readiness to hear and answer our prayers, made in Jesus' name?

- my experience since acknowledging God as real, and loving, has repeatedly demonstrated that prayer results in improvements in my life, or in a new insight into how God wants us to live in the relationship between Him and us: I live much of the rest of my life on the basis of what I learn from experience – why not this part as well?

2 All prayer is our means of communication with our unseeable God; our process of letting Him into our souls. However,

- when we pray with other people's words (e.g. led by a minister in a formal service, or following the words in the Scriptures or a prayerbook or set liturgy) we are taking advantage of the experience and learning of the authors of those words to guide us to recognise and/or remind us of particular truths about the nature of God and of the situations which we are facing in our earthly lives.

- when we pray in our own words we are crying out to God in praise or request, in faith that He will hear prayers made in the name of Jesus Christ (even though we may not expect, or even recognise, His answers, and though those answers will come in His good time, not ours).

- when we pray in contemplation of a work of art we are seeking to identify those aspects of God's glory and greatness and love for which the object can remind us to give Him praise.

- when we pray in silence we try to still our over-active minds and tongues, so that there might be no obstruction to our souls' receipt of God's incoming messages to us.

~~~~~~

Prayer for me has become a kind of meditation, not in a yoga sense, but quiet thinking and occasional mantra prayers, thinking things through. It has very little to do with the formal prayers at church. I find the idea of petitioning very strange – I remember teaching sailing on an International Student Christian Fellowship cruise and being expected to pray for sunshine and fine weather when the farms around us in Norfolk were in drought conditions. I was thinking, there are probably some Christians around here praying for rain! I find it difficult, though, because I do want to pray for peace, for example, but I don't think there's going to be a kind of big hand out of the sky sorting things out, no Red Sea parting for the Israelis and Palestinians. We, as humans, have brought these things on ourselves and there's no easy answer. On the one hand, I do wonder if prayer is simply meditating on peace, and unless we get up and do something and make our views known then nothing will change. On the other hand, I do appreciate the times when people who are ill are prayed for. I see it as a communal remembering and being part of a family.

On the whole, though, prayer for me is private wrestling, thought and personal anguish, meditation. I'm not a quiet person – I'm a busy person, with a need for quiet. I tend to write poems and make paintings in series, a few weeks of hectic activity then two weeks mooching around. I feel refuelled by getting a buzz going but I also need to slow down and listen to music and be quiet. There are moments when I need to think things through and I do turn to God in difficult times.

I know that there's something more than aesthetics or architecture to the church, there is a presence. I believe there is a deity and that there was an incarnation of God on this earth that mended a relationship, though I don't quite understand how. For me, God is something outside myself, not something I've created. God is a powerful being who created this world. I believe most of the creed and I think there's something more than just this world.

Of course it's not at all provable on an intellectual level, I'm not sold on any of the theologians who say you can definitely prove that God exists by arguing this. There has to be a kind of leap of faith or doubt. I've always seen it as swings and round-abouts – that faith and doubt go hand in hand.

▄▄▄▄▄

1 I don't know. I was struck by Rowan Williams in a radio conversation before becoming Archbishop of Canterbury, that he has this perhaps strange idea that 'prayer works'. It was a Brains Trust programme, so 'reason' was to the fore. I don't know what 'works' might mean; people don't automatically get well if prayed for, the world doesn't become peaceful because prayers are made for it to be so. The effect on the pray-er may be significant; perhaps tele-pathic goodwill, and direct, everyday goodwill from the effort of prayer, has some meaning.

2 I imagine I am engaging in something of the above, funda-mentally a benign process, and with others a connecting-with-each-other one. Clearly praying together can also be routine, complacent, self-serving, etc., so it's not a clear-cut case.

3 The question assumes I believe or even know that there are 'results' in some tangible form. I find myself saying to myself, 'here we are on this planet spinning in space, what the hell does it mean, what's it for?' That's to say, I can see prayer as an instinctive calling out, crying out, exclaiming, and it goes with a consciousness of the strangeness of 'being alive', of 'being a person'.

4 Communal prayer is apparently easy enough, whether one is leading it or being spoken for, or whether it is being spoken together. Regular and disciplined private prayer as commonly understood I have always found very hard, and

have not for the most part practised it. The questions that follow elicit (perhaps) pertinent other responses.

5 My sense of myself making poems, and also when painting pictures, making montages and so on, is sometimes one of 'being taken out of myself, of 'being subsumed to a purpose'. Years ago I began to mistrust what seemed easy momentary emotion induced by, say, particular pieces or moments of music, or of a wonderful landscape, or indeed in response to something in someone else's experience; these moments seem certainly cumulative and contribute to what one's life is, but don't seem to me in themselves reliable.

6 Thomas Cranmer's Collects stay with me, notably the final prayer of Evening Prayer and of Compline ('Lighten our darkness'), diminished, I think, by the people who wrote the new version now in use. There was a time when I took to saying the Hail Mary, because I needed to: I don't know who wrote that. St Francis of Assisi's 'Lord make me an instrument of your peace' was ruined for me when Margaret Thatcher used it when elected. Jesus is said to have given us the Lord's Prayer.

7 It depends on one's definition and understanding of prayer. It seems too easy to say this poem, that cantata, that painting, is as close to a prayer as one can get; but yet the question draws on our true experience. Last year I wrote poems in response to George Rouault's 58 etchings, **Miserere et Guerre**; the poems were commissioned by Birmingham Museum and Art Gallery, and it meant I spent many hours with Rouault's work; this 'staying with' someone else's art was as concentrated an experience of that kind as I've had, and I would say now he seems to have been in some kind of state of what one might call prayer when making those pictures.

8 I don't think I've been consistent enough to have made a decisive giving up. But after attending my local parish church for many years, sometimes regularly, sometimes less so – and I think it's a good example of what a parish church can be – I have lately come to feel that Jesus would not have been there but would have been on the High

Street, in hospitals, where people work, rather than in the church, and I have stopped attending. So I have dropped out of traditional communal prayer.

9 Yes, of course! And it seems no coincidence that monks and nuns often seem to have as bright and sharp a wit as anyone, often more so.

10 This is the hardest question of all, because it throws my life wide open, out of which opening there must be much I'd find myself saying about prayer. What I came to like about church services, and when I was a young curate I once preached on 'Jesus the surrealist', was coming out into the High Street afterwards and seeing everything afresh again – and strange. Prayer perhaps reminds us we are mortal, and frail, as well as having the possibility of love and creative endeavour.

~~~~~~~

1 It doesn't have to be. Important though rational thought is, there are a lot of areas of human life and experience – feeling, imagination, creativity – which it does not encompass. Having said that, to go aside, to be alone and quiet, to try to put your experience into a wider perspective and be open to what may come from beyond yourself, is an entirely reasonable thing to do.

2 Trying to give free and honest expression to my own thoughts and feelings, and then trying to let myself be open to any comeback or insight from beyond myself – to be open to the Other who can confront us in the depths of our being.

3 Responses to prayer can be at least as many and various as the possible responses to our approaching another person. It's no good trying to manipulate God. The response may, or may not, be one we want to hear. The more ready we are to be challenged, the more dramatic may be the results.

4 How hard is it to write poetry or hit a cricket ball? To be any good takes constant practice. Sometimes we may enjoy

that, and seem to be doing well. Sometimes it may be the very last thing we want to do, and will feel a waste of time. Working through the bad patches is what can bring the real rewards.

5 What you do with your body is important. Time spent getting yourself relaxed and centred, steadying your breathing, calming your mind – all this can be part of prayer, not just its preliminary. Walk, sit, kneel, dance; all can be part of prayer.

6 Yes.

7 Yes, many. Whether you respond to any in that way depends on the individual, time, mood, circumstance. Writing poetry, for instance, draws on some of the same resources as prayer – a search for inner truthfulness, in relation to an outward reference point, quiet, concentration, confession sometimes. It is not the same as prayer, but a discipline to which you give yourself wholly can certainly be part of your spirituality.

8 Probably not deliberately – though sometimes through laziness, or similar reasons.

9 Interesting question! Joy and laughter certainly can be. Humour often is about the contradictions we get caught in, about our mixed feelings, the ways we get compromised. Prayer is an important means of finding our way through these things, being honest with ourselves, finding integrity. So, perhaps, you could say that humour can be a starting point for prayer, showing where some of the confusions lie. Prayer can also lead us to laugh at ourselves sometimes.

〰〰〰

1 If God is a person then it seems rational to speak/listen to him. This is the normal way we build relationships.

2 I believe that, apart from all the human and very mixed motives involved, I am making myself available to God at the deepest level. What happens after that is his business.

3 I have experienced very concrete and surprising answers to specific, material requests, but the real, ongoing answers

are about my changing character which is noticed more often by other people, and can just seem like silence to me.

4 Very – except at certain periods when praying is like taking draughts of wine. Most of the time, it is a discipline.

5 I use gesture sometimes (genuflection, making the sign of the cross, bowing) and I use dance. I lead a circle dance group at church each week, which is about bringing the body into a rhythmic freedom and centres the mind/spirit with others. Some dances are explicitly religious/Christian, others are not, but they arrive at the same centring state.

6 I often remember St Richard's prayer, 'Jesus, friend and brother, may I see thee more clearly, love thee more dearly, follow thee more nearly, day by day' (I know that isn't the whole thing), and St Ignatius's 'serve and not to ask for any reward' prayer. I also use the Orthodox 'Jesus Prayer'.

7 I should think most works of art/music, etc., are prayer, in the sense that the creative parts of us are those that are open to inspiration (Spirit). But like prayers, they communicate that to others more or less convincingly.

8 Yes – as a very hurt and disturbed teenager, when the adults in my life seemed impervious to my faith, or anyone else's. I think I felt that I couldn't beat them, so I had better join them. It lasted about two years.

9 I occasionally hear God having a joke at my expense . . . so I think he appreciates mine.

◆◆◆◆◆

1 I think if you believe in a loving, communicating God, talking to him is most rational.

2 When I pray I am talking to my Father who cares and is interested, who gives me succour and encouragement.

3 There is always a 'response' but not necessarily the response you are expecting. God also has a habit of being so cryptic it borders on the obscure. Sometimes looking back in hindsight I can see clearly how He responded; yet I could not see it at the time. Sometimes, His answers are crystal clear whether they be guiding or just plain com-

forting. Sometimes He simply says 'no' – which is the hardest thing to accept when you are praying for something specific. His 'no' is easily interpreted as silence, but is usually a prelude to something else far more spectacular.

4   I find it hard to pray out loud in a home group, but can readily write a formal prayer for the service at St Mary's and pray it out loud in front of the whole congregation. At home I pray in the evening (to go through my day) and in the morning (to help me get through my day): these prayers are very personal and informal, as I would pray to my Father.

5   I tend to pray only with words.

6   Sadly I cannot name a prayer composed by someone else.

7   I find nature in its various forms of magnificence is close to a prayer in itself. Earlier this week as I drew my curtains there were black, menacing snow clouds. The dawn was piercing the clouds, stabbing them through deep red. It looked like the sky was on fire, in God's glory.

8   I walked away from God for a long time and did not pray. My life was a mess, He did not care, He did not listen and He was not there. Of course He was there, I was just choosing to ignore Him. When I chose His way my life was not quite the life I anticipated, but a far more contented and fulfilled one.

9   I have learnt through the twists and turns of my life that God has an extremely ironic sense of humour. I don't think He minds if we use irony and humour in our prayers.

10   There is no right and wrong way to pray. Different people pray in different ways. Different circumstances call for different styles of prayer. How you pray is whatever works for you. What matters is your bond to Him, His bond to you. How you create that bond is almost an irrelevance so long as it brings you closer to Him.

⋙⋙

1   Rational, yes.

2   Since sound waves can alter matter, I think thought waves can do the same.

3 Results or responses can be visible but more likely invisible. And who knows about timescales or purpose?

4 Very hard to keep it fresh, open and alive.

5 Watching Michael Jackson writing music with his dance, I wondered about this. Creating music and art can be prayer depending on the thoughts going into it, I think.

6 It's snippets that remain in my memory. Robert Herricks' child and his 'paddocks'. George Herbert's poem on prayer, calling it 'reversed thunder'. A lovely child's prayer about praying for creatures who love the wet, particularly ducks, which I have copied out somewhere and haven't got time to find for you. Gerald Manley Hopkins' 'dappled things'.

7 The Taj Mahal. I think the architect caught some amazing inner harmony.

8 I've only recently come to taking prayer really seriously and believing in it, though have always been associated with a church.

9 Wit and humour, yes. Not sure about irony. Like satire, it's enjoyable but has the touch of cruelty. How much should one flay hypocrisy?!

10 For me, in landscape and the open air are the easiest places to pray. Woods, hills and the sea. Even in the garden. And by myself. I think the highlight of my life was sunrise in the Himalayas with its vastness of space, silence and colour. Out of this world.

~~~~~

1 I think the concept of prayer and praying is rational in the deepest sense. To have discourse with one's creator is a need felt in the furthest reaches of a man's soul. How sensible, then, to respond to that need.

2 When I pray alone, I have a private audience with a kind and benevolent king. When I pray with others, I form a special bond with those people, not unlike a friend who bragged to me that she had once smoked with a well-known musician.

3 I think the only result one can count on, if one is a believer,

is a tiny bit of growth in his relationship with God, with each utterance in prayer.

4 Sometimes prayer comes as easily as breathing, at other times, it's the hardest thing in the world.

5 No.

6 'The serenity prayer' by St Francis.

7 In my experience, the drawings of Christ on the cross by Michelangelo are close to being prayers, as are many songs (and performances) by the late Rich Mullins.

8 I've deliberately given up praying several times, only to find that God still had me in his net, and it's useless to ignore him.

9 If a person truly believes that wit, irony or humour are okay in prayer, then I suppose they are. But if you don't believe it, God knows you don't, and it's probably not a good idea to play games with him.

10 I believe that prayer is one of the most important activities a person can engage in, and wish I had the attention span to pray twice as much as I do.

~~~~~

1 For me, prayer comes almost exclusively at two distinct times: one is entirely irrational, at times of crisis; the other is entirely rational, at times of celebration. Thankfully, most of my prayers are celebratory ones at present.

2 I pray alone occasionally, but consider the singing, music making and poetry performance I do to be a form of invocation, akin to prayer, and that is an entirely shared experience. What do I believe I'm doing? Celebrating life, channelling energy, being affirmative with and in the presence of others.

3 Responses are always surprising, not because I believe someone or thing has 'heard' my prayer and responded, but because the idea of the godhead, for me, is a tension between the outer and inner worlds. Responses then are generated entirely from this tension; they come from within, but provoked from without. Responses to prayer

are a part of self. They are, if you like, paradoxically both logical and illogical ways of problem solving.

4 Not as hard as it is to love unconditionally.

5 Yes, with music and singing and sometimes with tears.

6 'How Much Longer Will I Be Able to Inhabit the Divine Sepulchre', a poem by John Ashbery.

7 The Taj Mahal, a 'teardrop on the face of humanity'.

8 No, because I never deliberately ever set out to pray in the first place, it's an organic process. I don't like the strictures of 'never' doing something again; I prefer the organic middle path.

9 Yes, more tea, Vicar?

10 It is something I always anticipate a personal need for but find it difficult to rationalise – writing about prayer is a bit like dancing about architecture.

DISCOVERING
FAITH
THROUGH Different
voices

Different Voices

In this final section to **Sounding Heaven and Earth** different perspectives in the form of discussion points have been drawn up for individual and group consideration.

An overall purpose is to attempt to achieve a stronger idea of why prayers and praying are still so significant in a world of secular noise and spiritual adversity.

The forms that prayer take are also important, particularly when traditional expressions are perceived by many young people to be adorned by other voices, other times; rituals that simply do not relate to what needs to be said today.

The discussion points are accordingly based on objectives and approaches, enhancements, the challenges of prayer and the voices of prayer. How do we find our own voices and approaches within a ceaseless stream of sounds?

The Different Voices of Prayers

The following are suggested topics for discussion.

The objectives and approaches to your own praying

- When you pray are you mostly asking for things, for yourself or for others? Are you celebrating? Are you attempting to work things out?
- Do you sometimes pray out of fear, or in anger or in doubt?
- Do you sometimes simply set about praying out of habit?
- Is prayer a different thing depending on whether you pray by yourself or within a group?
- When a prayer is read or led by somebody else, does this reduce or enhance its impact on you?
- Select a prayer in this anthology. When you have read it and fully considered its objective, what do you think it expects of you? What do you need to do to make it more meaningful? What responsibility do you have for a prayer?
- Are there moments in your life when prayer is impossible? Why is this so? What do you do about it?
- Are there some things that cannot or should not be mentioned in prayers?
- Do you have to believe in God in order to pray?
- Are there subconscious prayers, more meditative than organized, more pure emotion than rational?

- Have you ever considered or used a Prayer Plan to better engage in regular and committed praying?
- What is your view of praying not only about the dead but for the dead?
- What is your view of praying for animals?
- At what moments and on what occasions is silence the best help to prayer?

Enhancing prayers

- Have there been occasions when music, art, a building or a passage of writing have themselves become something close to a prayer? Can such things actually be prayers?
- Are you aware of the vocabulary you use in your own prayers? Is anything distinct about your language? For example, is the language slightly archaic? Do you repeat words or phrases?
- How do you know when a prayer has reached its conclusion?
- Can the music and lyrics of popular songs such as 'We Shall Overcome' become an actual prayer?
- Do you send prayers to other people? Do you e-mail prayers? Do you pray on the telephone? Do you discuss your prayers with your friends?
- Has belief in God led you to praying or have you discovered God within the act of praying?
- When you pray, how important is the ritual? Do you need to kneel down, to place your hands together, to bow your head, to close your eyes? Do you find just the opposite to be helpful: standing up, raising your open hands, holding hands, raising your face, raising your voice?
- Have you ever painted a prayer, danced a prayer, sung a prayer, acted out a prayer?

Jesus and prayer

- What specific things do you receive from The Lord's Prayer? Is this for you the foundation prayer, the prayer of all prayers?
- Are there specific moments in the life of Christ that you can relate to when you pray? When you are challenged? When you are afraid? When you are tempted? When you need to forgive?
- Of all the things that Jesus taught us and left for us to follow, why is prayer so important?
- Could you as a Christian not be active in praying?

Challenges

- How can we deal with the problem of pain in prayer?
- Can one pray properly in anger?
- If a prayer is too easily made, does it have any real power?
- What do you think an 'answer' to a prayer might be?
- How do you pray for somebody you dislike? How do you pray for somebody who wishes you harm? How could you pray for a person who bullies you?

The Different Voices of Poetry

The following are suggested topics for discussion.

Religious poems

- Can you think of a poem that to your mind appears to be a prayer? Is there an example in this book?
- Select some passages from the Bible that appear to be nearer to poetry than prose.
- What do you expect of a religious poem?
- Are there examples of lyrics to popular songs that you would regard as spiritual poems?
- Does a poem have to mean to be?
- How important is the sound of a poem?
- Are there hymns that you consider to be poems?
- Can you distinguish between a 'spiritual' poem and a 'religious' poem?

Poems in your life

- At what moments of your life has a complete poem or a passage of poetry summed up your state of mind?
- Are there some poems that have been a major influence on your faith? Have they challenged your belief? Have they enhanced it?

- Have there been times in your life when, attempting to sort things out, you have written a poem or something very close to a poem? Is this because the form or discipline of the writing provided a much needed challenge? Is it because you wanted to express yourself in a totally different way?
- Are you prepared not to fully understand a poem in the same way that you may not always fully appreciate other works of art: music, painting, sculpture, ballet?

The role of religious poems

- Are religious poems ever read in your school assembly or church or in your RE lessons?
- Is there a place for anger, politics or protest in religious poetry?
- Could a poem be painted or danced or sung or acted?
- Is there such a thing as a silent poem?

Reading

- In the Introduction to this anthology there are the names of some writers who have prayed from the very darkest places, facing a light they knew was still there: Bonhoeffer, Celan, Gershon, Wiesel and Levi. There are also the names of several poets. There are many more to be found in individual collections and in poetry anthologies.
- In addition there are collections of traditional Native American literature, Celtic poetry and prayers and numerous voices from writers and priests who have been imprisoned for their beliefs.

The Different
Voices of Prose

The following are suggested topics for discussion.

- Both 'The Wife's Story' and 'The Relay' work on different levels. They have a clear story-line and then it becomes apparent that something else is happening and this reshapes the entire narrative.
- What more can you find out about the concept and tradition of 'holy fools'?
- Do you know of other stories that are based on a biblical account or theme?
- Can you recall passages of prose or scenes from stage plays or films that retain special spiritual importance for you?
- Have there been paintings or photographs or pieces of sculpture or music that have a spiritual dimension that has impressed you?
- There are plays, films and novels that have expressed problems and protested accordingly. Do you believe that art can change things and that words in particular can make things happen?
- The reflections of Wanda Nash about prayer and laughter, prayer and playing, may promote other thoughts. Are there other approaches we should consider? Might some of them be of particular relevance to young people, those who feel isolated, those who distrust or dislike the decorum and ritual in traditional forms of worship?

- Bruce Bitmead's prose poems surprise and make us think again. What do these intense passages mean to you?
- How might we encounter God in other ways: in gardens, in forests, on mountain tops and in deserts, in a display of flowers, in sport, in intellectual challenges, in the midst of pain or grief or war, in other forms and voices and words?
- Is there a place in your memory or a place that you can still visit that means for you 'nearest to heaven'? Why is this place so meaningful?
- Is it possible to confuse the emotionally uplifting with the spiritual? What do we mean when we call such inspirations and talents 'God given'?
- Letters, diaries, autobiographies and biographies are capable of expressing moments of revelation and spiritual truth. Can you think of such writing that comes from a background of extreme danger, stress or hardship?

Different Voices
Connecting

The following are suggested topics for discussion.

The Passion portrayals

- The life, times and death of Jesus have been portrayed in thousands of creative works. They have more than painted a picture. They have inspired, changed lives, founded values, provided a reason for living. Some of these works of art have challenged, provoked anger and protest. Why in particular are both Christians and non-Christians so drawn to the days leading up to the killing of Christ on a cross?
- What distinct elements of the Passion story lend themselves to dramatic presentations, or music, or dance, or poetry, or sculpture?
- Do betrayal, trial, torture, killing the Messiah, resurrection, belong to any other non-Christian religions?

Treatment

- What for you is the most revealing phrase or image, metaphor or meaning, in the two poem sequences and/or the images by E. Charlotte Wright?
- Consider writing a script for radio or television about the journey to crucifixion. Focus on the actual events, the stop-

ping places, the small details, the people and what they see and say, relating it to the sequence by Tony Lucas.

- In the paintings by E. Charlotte Wright, what do you feel about the presence of present-day people such as President Bush and President Putin, a paedophile, David Beckham, and a small child in Delhi? What are they doing here? What does their presence do to the meaning of the sequence?
- Focus on the body bag. What does this image mean to you? Victim 37 – what makes a person do this?
- In the final poem of David H. W. Grubb's sequence there is a complete narrative demonstrating determination and a strength to survive. Set within an African conflict, in the presence of Irish nuns, the young boy represents the future. How does this single poem relate to the 'Stations of the Cross' work as a whole, the concept of Tony Lucas and E. Charlotte Wright and David H. W. Grubb? How can beliefs from the past and the present and the future connect? How is this essential to the Christian message?

The Different Voices of Music and Dance

The following are suggested topics for discussion.

- In many faiths music and dance form part of the individual and group worship. In what ways might Christian worship make greater use of both?
- What great works of religious music can you refer to? On what level do they work? Are they capable of more than raising the pulse and spirit?
- What makes some works of religious music sublime? Are there moments when music can take the human mind beyond normal expression and feeling?
- Choral works, anthems, operas, requiems; have these musical feasts become art and more secular and less spiritual for any specific reasons? What sort of a challenge is this to living Christians?
- Are there specific reasons why dance is perceived as a less valuable element in Christian expression? What might its current role be in terms of telling biblical stories, parables, the narratives of Christ's life, the work and significance of prophets, disciples, saints, etc.?
- Are there theological objections to dance?
- If most young people engage in music and dance what

implications should there be for churches, Christian youth clubs, etc.?

- Dance as praise; dance as prayer; dance as exploration; dance as doubt; dance as revelation; what special powers might dance have and in what ways might dance be reintroduced to individual and group worship?

Dance and drama themes: Biblical

The Creation Stories
Advent
Christmas
Lent
Easter
The Seasons
Miracles
The Flood
The Lord's Prayer
Lazarus

Dance and drama themes: Issues

Poverty
War
The Environment
Bullying
Old Age
Marriage
Prejudice
Trust

Sources and Acknowledgements

We thank all those who have given us permission to reproduce extracts from publications in this book, as indicated in the list below. Every effort has been made to trace copyright ownership. The publisher would be grateful to be informed of any omissions.

CAFOD: **Buried Grain**.

Children's Aid Direct: **A Child's Prayer** and **For the Children**.

England, Gerald: **He Who Would Speak**, published in **Christian Living**, USA; **Prayer**, published in **Tait's Quarterly**, Orkney; **SQUARE 8g**, published in **Printed Matter**, Japan.

Gallagher, Katherine: **Chartres Cathedral** and **Put Your Hands Into Fire**, published in **Passages To The City**, Australia.

Grubb, David H. W.: **Stations**, published in a SPIRE Trust booklet.

Hadfield, Charles: **Anything Could Happen**, published in **Border Disputes**, Salzburg, 1995; **Hope Cove**, published in **Inventing Waterfalls**, Salzburg, 1997.

Loydell, Rupert M: **Gregorian Chants**, published in **Fill These Days**, Stride, 1990, and **Frosted Light: Fourteen**

Sequences, 1978–1988, University of Salzburg Press, 1996. **Holy Places**, published in **Between Dark Dreams,** Acumen Books, 1992. **Touching Truth**, published in **Timbers Across The Sun**, University of Salzburg Press, 1993. **Visitation**, published in **Home All Along**, Chrysalis Poetry, 1999.

Lucas, Tony: **Stations**, published in 2003 as a Southwark pamphlet.

Nash, Wanda: **Come Let Us Play**, DLT, 1999.

Pearce, Brian Louis: **Credo**, published in **Leaving the Corner**, Stride, 1992, and in **Gwen John Talking**, Tallis, 1985; **Third Way**, published in **Coeli Et Terra**, Cornerstone, USA, 1993.

Pritchard, The Rt Revd John: **Circle Us** and **Litany of Jesus**, published in the **Intercessions Handbook**, SPCK, 1997.

Ramsay, Jay: **Prayer at Sheepscombe**, published in **Kingdom of the Edge – New and Selected Poems**, Element, 1999; **Spire**, published in **Acumen** magazine.

Rimbaud, Dee: **Dream Eclipses Reality**, published in **My Mum's a Punk**, Scottish Children's Press anthology; **Iona Meditation**, published in **Helicon**; **La Que Sabe's Bell**, published in **Pennine Platform**.

Satyamurti, Carole: **The White Room**, published in the **Interpreter House** magazine and the anthology **We Have Come Through**, Bloodaxe, 2003.

Simms, Gordon: **In the Walled Garden**, published by Ragged Raven Press; **The Sounds of Islay**, published by Thomas The Mill.

Simpson, Matt: **Funerary Monuments, Aegina**, published in **Getting There**, Liverpool University Press, 2001; **The Song of Caedmon**, published in **Making Arrangements**, Bloodaxe, 1982; **An Elegy for Galosherman**, Bloodaxe, 1990.

Skinner, Susan: **A Grace Before Nature** and **New Year**, published in **Graces for Today**, John Hunt.

SOURCES AND ACKNOWLEDGEMENTS

The SPIRE Trust: The SPIRE Trust prayers are taken from services written for churches and schools: **Alphabets of Light** (Education Sunday), **Saints Sunday** (All Saints), **An Advent Gathering** and **Do They Know It's Easter?**, published in 2002 and 2003.

Topping, Angela: **She Considers Sea Burial**, published in **The Fiddle**, Stride, 1999; **Tending the Plot**, published in **Dandelions For Mother's Day**, Stride, 1989.

Waddington-Feather, John: **The Daily Creator Prayer**, published in **The Poetry Church Magazine**.

Whitehead, Wendy: **Mary's Month**, published by The Ecumenical Society of the Blessed Virgin Mary, 1997; **A General Thanksgiving**, adapted from a contribution to **Prayers for Peace**, D. Ben Rees (ed.), Fellowship of Reconciliation.

Working At the Cutting Edge

Working at local community level with specially recruited and trained volunteers, The SPIRE Trust supports pupils in religious education at secondary school level. Its main role is to provide 'living Christians' who can assist teachers in responding to real issues in a practical and relevant manner. This is done through pupil conferences, workshops and extended assemblies. Responding to the needs of LEAs and individual schools and the introduction of Citizenship, it intends to develop its pupil conference work significantly.

Chief Executive David Grubb, previously an RE teacher and headteacher, expresses the distinct role of SPIRE in this way: 'We want to promote dialogue and create a focus for faith within the highly demanding and structured school day. RE needs to be relevant and real. It needs to feel right. That's why music, drama and creative expression are vital factors in the way issues are explored, and the SPIRE team needs to be made up of people who have personal experience not just expertise.'

'Cutting Edge Conferences' are designed to maximise pupil participation in response to key issues such as prejudice, medical ethics, the environment, war, euthanasia, abortion, science and faith, and challenges to Christians.

The SPIRE Trust works on the basis of what could be called 'The Four Rs'. It believes that RE in secondary schools needs to be relevant, real, right and revealing. To be **relevant** the experience of RE must be set in the context of today, the

172

current scene, the challenges and catastrophes and sheer excitement of the twenty-first century. This involves problem solving, calls to action, examining how information is handled.

To be **real** in the minds and lives of young people RE needs to be primarily about people, in particular young people. It too often appears to be about ritual, roles, texts and tribes.

The third R is to do with secondary school pupils feeling **right** with the subject matter, the way it is presented and the position it places them in as individuals and group members. If RE doesn't switch them on it could be because they are suspicious, feel exposed to what they perceive to be attempts to evangelise, or feel that the subject expects too much. The problem of articulation and communication is immense in a subject that does not appear to be like any other subject.

The fourth R is the greatest challenge of all. RE appears to be massively concerned with other people's revelations, an ancient tapestry of other people's narratives. What about **self-revelation**? School pupils will only find the geater meaning and experience of RE if they are encouraged to express their ideas in their own voices. The texts, music, poetry, dance and drama of their own youth culture have to be trusted to deliver the lesson of RE. Discussion, dialogue, listening to what pupils believe in or don't believe in lies at the heart of the matter.

For all these reasons The SPIRE Trust is researching new ways of working, new ways of presentation, new forms of engagement.

The SPIRE Trust has created four dynamic services for use in churches and schools: for Education Sunday, Lent, All Saints and Advent. There will be additional thematic and interactive services forthcoming.

For further information about The SPIRE Trust visit our website on www.spiretrust.org.uk or contact David Grubb, 76a St Marks Road, Henley-on-Thames, Oxon, RG9 1LW.

Index of Titles and First Lines

INDEX OF TITLES AND FIRST LINES

INDEX OF TITLES AND FIRST LINES

INDEX OF TITLES AND FIRST LINES

INDEX OF TITLES AND FIRST LINES

INDEX OF TITLES AND FIRST LINES

INDEX OF TITLES AND FIRST LINES

INDEX OF TITLES AND FIRST LINES

Index of Authors

INDEX OF AUTHORS

INDEX OF AUTHORS

Index of Themes and Subjects

INDEX OF THEMES AND SUBJECTS